The GREATEST BAD MOVIES of ALL TIME

The GREATEST BAD MOVIES of ALL TIME

by Phil Hall

BearManor Media

2013

The Greatest Bad Movies of All Time

© 2013 Phil Hall

All rights reserved.

For information, address:

BearManor Media
P. O. Box 71426
Albany, GA 31708

bearmanormedia.com

Typesetting and layout by John Teehan
Cover photo: Elisa Ferrari

CASABLANCA serigraph © Melanie Taylor Kent, LTD.

Published in the USA by BearManor Media

ISBN—1-59393-731-8
978-1-59393-731-7

*For everyone who ever encouraged me—
my eternal thanks!*

*For everyone who ever discouraged me—
I hate to tell you this, but you were wrong!*

Table of Contents

Acknowledgments xi
Introduction 1
Abbott and Costello Go to Mars 5
The Adventures of Ford Fairlane 7
The Adventures of Pluto Nash 9
Airport 1975 11
Alice of Wonderland in Paris 13
All This and World War II 15
At Long Last Love 17
Atoll K 19
The Babe Ruth Story 21
Battlefield Earth 23
Beat the Devil 25
Beyond the Sea 27
The Bible: In The Beginning 29
Birdemic: Shock and Terror 31
The Black Cauldron 33
Black Devil Doll From Hell 35
The Blue Bird 37
Boys Beware 39
Bubble 41
The Buster Keaton Story 43
Butterfly 45
*Can Heironymus Merkin Ever Forget Mercy Humppe
  and Find True Happiness?* 47

The Cat in the Hat	49
Catwoman	51
Chariots of the Gods	53
Che!	55
Christabel	57
The Conqueror	59
The Creeping Terror	61
Dance Hall Racket	63
A Dirty Shame	65
Dogarama	67
Don's Plum	71
Don't Worry, We'll Think of a Title	73
The Dragon Lives Again	75
The Driver's Seat	77
Empire	79
The Fat Spy	83
Fear and Desire	85
Gamera	87
The Giant Claw	89
Gigli	91
Godzilla vs. Megalon	93
Goodbye, Norma Jean	95
The Green Cockatoo	97
Hammersmith Is Out	101
Harvard Man	105
Head	107

Health 109

The Hottie & the Nottie 113

Hugo the Hippo 115

The Human Centipede (First Sequence) 117

If Footmen Tire You, What Will Horses Do? 119

In Old Chicago 121

Inchon 123

The Iron Petticoat 125

The Jazz Singer 127

Joan Rivers: A Piece of Work 129

King Lear 131

Klezmer on Fish Street 133

The Last of the Secret Agents? 135

Lost Horizon 137

The Maltese Bippy 141

Mame 143

Manos, the Hands of Fate 147

The Merchant of Venice 151

Mr. Arkadin 153

Mr. Freedom 155

Moment by Moment 157

Mother Riley Meets the Vampire 159

Mommie Dearest 161

Mourning Becomes Electra 165

Move 167

Mystic River 169

The Negro Soldier 173
Paul McCartney Really Is Dead: The Last Testament of
    George Harrison? 177
Plan 9 from Outer Space 179
Reefer Madness 181
Renaldo and Clara 183
The Room 187
Santa Claus 191
Santa Claus Conquers the Martians 193
Sextette 195
Sh! The Octopus 199
Shanghai Surprise 201
Song of Norway 203
Staircase 205
Starcrash 207
A Streetcar Named Desire 209
Teenagers from Outer Space 213
The Terror 215
The Terror of Tiny Town 217
Triple Trouble 219
The Turkish Wizard of Oz 223
Valley of the Dolls 225
Visit to a Small Planet 229
The Wild, Wild World of Jayne Mansfield 233
The Wild World of Batwoman 23
Wizard of Oz 237
Zabriskie Point 241

Acknowledgments

WRITING IS NOT, by any stretch, a solitary labor. A number of fine people have influenced the creation of this book and this page is designed to pay thanks for their input.

You would not be reading this book had it not been for Ben Ohmart and his wonderful BearManor Media. This is my third book under the BearManor Media banner and I am grateful for being part of this wonderful team.

Special thanks are in order to Dominick Montalto for copyediting the manuscript.

Several of the essays in this book have appeared in earlier formats on a number of cinema appreciation websites. Thus, I extend my thanks to the creative forces behind these sites for supporting my writing over the past few years: Mark Bell of Film Threat, Kevin Mark Kline of EDGE Boston, Nic Baisley of FilmSnobbery.com, Matt Borondy of Identity Theory, and Kent Turner of Film-Forward.com.

A special appreciation is offered to some wonderful people who have provided extraordinary support and encouragement. They are, in alphabetical order, Antero Alli, Hadria Douglas, Robert Firsching, Chris Gore, Joe Kane, Ken Lee, Michael Legge, Nell Minow, Randy Pitman, Steve Puchalski, Eric Robichaud, Eric Michael Schraeder, Thomas Edward Seymour, Matthew Sorrento, Jimmy Traynor, Betty Jo Tucker, Mike Watt, Michael Wiese, and Felix Vasquez, Jr.

And my mother and my bro Theo get a special shout-out!

Introduction

"My great concern is not whether you have failed, but whether you are content with your failure."

— Abraham Lincoln

THE OVERWHELMING MAJORITY OF FILMS, I am sorry to say, are not very good. Indeed, for every classic film that emerges, there are scores of mediocre films that briefly emerge and quickly disappear without making much of an impact.

But every now and then, a film comes along that is so bad that it rises above the realm of mere mediocrity and attracts attention for its sheer awfulness. The noise resulting from these misfires creates a sensation, albeit not the type envisioned by those responsible for these works. I like to refer to these works as "anti-classics"—they have become part of the popular culture, yet their popularity is based on their ability to demolish cultural protocol.

In many ways, the anti-classics are the most fascinating films ever made. They defy easy classification and occupy multiple genres: highbrow art films that crash under their excessive pretension, comedies that fumble and stumble with an aggressive level of humorless antics, documentaries that offer a blatantly dishonest view of reality, lowbrow schlock that has no connection to the basic tenets of reality, musicals that crash into off-key shambles, and so forth.

It is quite a lopsided universe, to be certain. And, not unlike fingerprints, no two films are alike: each is wonderfully warped in its own twisted way. If there is a common ground, it comes via the audience's shock: it is hard to comprehend that such films exist.

Trying to harvest 100 of these anti-classics is arguably a thankless task. One could easily imagine an endless series of books on the topic with annual updates for the latest best-of-the-worst flicks. And considering the highly subjective nature of film criticism, there will be endless room for debate.

(But then again, the same could be said for a celebration of the classics—I know people who actively loathe *Gone with the Wind*, *Citizen Kane*, and *Casablanca* and are unimpressed with the countless books and articles advocating their greatness.)

Thus, I need to set the tone of this book by insisting it is *not* a be-all/end-all examination of the so-bad-it's-good movie orbit. This book is a work of opinion, not encyclopedic fact, and the reader has the right to disagree with the observations presented in the following pages. I am sure that more than a few readers will be puzzled by or object to the omission of a number of titles that have been widely considered by critics as representing the cinematic nadir. Some of these omissions are based on my belief that these titles have been unfairly maligned.

For example, the zany 1952 comedy *Bela Lugosi Meets a Brooklyn Gorilla* is absent even though mainstream film scholarship insists that it is among the worst comedies of all time. Perhaps the scholars dislike it, but I've screened the film for audiences on several occasions and the film never fails to entertain audiences—people laugh *with* the film's screwy humor, not at its alleged shortcomings.

Likewise, Michael Cimino's *Heaven's Gate* is not included here. I never shared the initial critical hostility that caused the expensive epic to crash and burn at the box office. I am happy to say that in the past few years, *Heaven's Gate* has grown in reputation and that many critics are now challenging the brutal reviews that first greeted the film at its disastrous New York premiere in November 1980.

Also missing are films that were roundly denounced by critics at the time of their release, but have since generated significant love from intense cult followings. Thus, if you are seeking the roller-skating musical *Xanadu*, the feather-ruffling absurdity of *Howard the Duck*, or the pole-dancing gyrations of *Showgirls*, you are in the wrong book.

Conversely, there are a few titles in this book that might baffle many people. A great many critics and film scholars would probably not think of including the Monkees' escapade *Head* or Clint Eastwood's award-winning *Mystic River* in a collection of this nature. But I believe that they are anti-classics and I offer my views on their acute shortcomings in this book.

In bringing together 100 films for this book, I also needed to establish some ground rules to ensure a rich exploration of the subject. First, I sought to limit the list to one entry per director. For some directors—particularly the notorious Edward D. Wood, Jr.—it would be too easy to include every film from their canon. This, of course, would require that several worthy titles be omitted. In Wood's case, his magnum opus *Plan 9 from Outer Space* is represented while his colorful mishaps *Glen or Glenda?* and *Bride of the Monster* are absent from the book. For Wood's contemporary Phil Tucker, I brought in *Dance Hall Racket* instead of his better-known *Robot Monster*. Yes, *Robot Monster* has the irresistible charm of a lunar invader played by a man wearing a gorilla suit and diving helmet, but in my view, *Dance Hall Racket* is more absurdly fascinating with an even more unlikely terrestrial presence: controversial comic Lenny Bruce in an unlikely dramatic role as a manic gangster.

Some genres, such as low-budget 1950s and 1960s horror/science fiction and the overproduced action/adventure thrillers of the past two decades, seem to be overpopulated with titles that are natural for inclusion here. While there is a very strong temptation to include a surplus of works featuring zipper-backed monsters stalking cardboard sets and CGI-heavy cacophonies costing hundreds of millions of dollars, I need to know where to draw the line, if only to achieve a degree of balance.

Furthermore, I am eager to diversify this discussion by offering works from a wide field of genres. There are several documentaries in this book—yes, even nonfiction filmmaking can result in works of daring ineptitude—and a couple of silent films are here to confirm that on-screen incompetence was alive and well before *The Jazz Singer* turned up. There is also a notoriously famous X-rated flick and even a student film—an unauthorized, truncated version of *A Streetcar Named Desire* (which includes a dance sequence to "Pennsylvania Polka").

I suspect that most of the films represented in this book will be familiar to readers, but there are some lesser-known films that may not ring that proverbial bell. If you've never heard of *Christabel* or *The Green Cockatoo* or *Hugo the Hippo*, you should consider yourself unlucky—you don't know what you're missing! These little films achieve a greater sense of deranged craziness than overstuffed duds like *The Garbage Pail Kids* or *Superbabies: Baby Geniuses 2*—and the latter two stinkers, I am glad to say, are not found beyond this sentence.

Also, the majority of the films being offered here are American-based productions. This is not to say that the United States has the world's worst film industry. In the cause of global brotherhood, I have included films from France, Germany, Great Britain, Hong Kong, Hungary, Italy, Japan, Mexico, Spain, Switzerland, and Turkey. I am sure there are plenty of anti-classics to be harvested from the frenzied film industries in China, India, Nigeria, and the Philippines, but I have yet to see enough of them to determine if they warrant inclusion here.

Ultimately, I wish to stress that this book is *not* designed to make fun of movies or to denigrate the efforts of creative artists. Nobody sets out with the goal of making a wonderfully terrible movie. Instead, I hope that this book can be seen as a celebration of films that somehow went down the wrong road and took up residence in a magnificent parallel universe where the well-established laws of logic, good taste, and coherence are unknown.

The films offered here truly deserve to be known as anti-classics—they *will* stand the test of time and continue to baffle, bemuse, and bother movie lovers for generations to come. Or at least until some smart-aleck film critic comes along and says, "Hey, wait a minute, these films aren't so bad after all!"

Abbott and Costello Go to Mars
(1953, directed by Charles Lamont)

IT APPEARS that no one at Universal-International was paying very much attention to this film's production since the title is utterly incorrect: Abbott and Costello travel to Venus, not Mars. But then again, if anyone had been actually paying much attention, this tired endeavor would have been cancelled before one frame of film was actually shot.

Lou Costello plays a childlike adult who is a resident at the Hideaway Orphans Home—no mean feat for a 47-year-old man who acts like an eight-year-old. Through contrived circumstances that bear no resemblance to real life, he winds up at a top-secret scientific facility, where courier-handyman Bud Abbott puts him to work. The duo wind up inside a rocket ship on the facility's launching pad and Costello accidentally hits a button that blasts them on a wild ride. The rocket lands in New Orleans during Mardi Gras, but Abbott and Costello take a look at the wild costumes worn by the revelers and mistakenly believe they are on an alien planet. Two escaped convicts hide on the rocket ship, which blasts off again for a trip to Venus and an encounter with a race of glamorous extraterrestrials played by the shapely contestants from the Miss Universe pageant.

Abbott and Costello began their film career in 1940 with supporting roles in the musical comedy *One Night in the Tropics*. Their first starring role in *Buck Privates* (1941) launched them through the 1940s with an output that included two to four movies a year plus a weekly radio series. By the 1950s, however, audiences had had more than enough of their antics and the pair's popularity began to sag as audiences looked away to the brash (and much younger) combination of Dean Martin and Jerry Lewis, who became the comedy team champs at the box office.

Part of the problem was the duo's material—they exhausted their beloved burlesque routines in their earlier films and were forced to slog through silly new film material through the late 1940s and early 1950s that barely fit their on-screen personas. Their lack of enthusiasm was too obvious during this period as most of their late-career films are stale. But the team was hardly played out—Abbott and Costello revived their well-worn routines for their television appearances and the energy they displayed in revisiting the old favorites on the small screen stood in stark contrast to the enervation they offered on the big screen.

In a weird way, *Abbott and Costello Go to Mars* resonates as an anti-comedy—a would-be mirthfest that is so aggressively unfunny that it generates laughs for the wrong reasons. Abbott's grouchy, distracted demeanor and his clear dislike for the childish material are actually funnier than Costello's desperate attempt to liven up the inane proceedings with his too-broad portrayal of a dimwitted man-child. The special effects are pure Z-grade, although the notion of having the Statue of Liberty duck from an oncoming rocket is cute.

And some retro charm can be found in the concept of an all-female planet (a plot twist that popped up a few times in the cheapo sci-fi flicks of the 1950s). Of course, eagle-eyed viewers can have their own spot-the-star fun in trying to locate a then-unknown Anita Ekberg as part of the Venusian cheesecake brigade.

The Adventures of Ford Fairlane
(1990, directed by Renny Harlin)

DURING THE 1980S and early 1990s, comic Andrew Dice Clay (born Andrew Clay Silverstein) enjoyed a considerable degree of notoriety for his scatological brand of stand-up humor. Clay's comedy created equal amounts of outrage and laughter. Although his concert appearances were sold out, detractors slammed the misogynist and racist nature of many of his routines.

Clay had scored several minor roles in a few 1980s films—most notably as a bouncer in the 1986 cult favorite *Pretty in Pink*—before his stand-up success enabled him to take charge of the leading role in Renny Harlin's 1990 *The Adventures of Ford Fairlane*. Playing a "rock and roll detective" with a Sunset Boulevard office, Clay's Fairlane finds himself in a music industry whodunit populated by B-level celebrities (Wayne Newton, Priscilla Presley, Gilbert Gottfried) and then-popular figures in fleeting cameo appearances (including Prince-guided performers Sheila E. and Morris Day and Robert Englund of the *Nightmare on Elm Street* series).

But the most fascinating aspect of *The Adventures of Ford Fairlane* ultimately was Clay's stunning inability to transfer his stage persona to the big screen. If anything, the camera magnified all of Clay's vices while obscuring whatever virtues he brought to the comedy scene.

Roger Ebert cogently observed that the cinematic lack of audience intimacy resulted in an entertainer adrift and exposed. "In a club or on a stage, foul-mouthed and race-baiting, he implicates the audience, and they laugh in order to exclude themselves as his targets (anyone who doesn't laugh is by definition an a- - - - - e)," Ebert wrote. "But a movie audience is more separate, more contemplative—and, sitting in the dark, watching him, more likely to be appalled than entertained."

However, not that many people bothered to show up to be appalled, let alone entertained. Dismal reviews and a weaker-than-expected box office gross doomed *The Adventures of Ford Fairlane* (domestically, it brought in a puny $21 million). The film's failure, coupled with the equally unsuccessful 1991 concert film *Dice Rules*, virtually derailed Clay's career.

Despite numerous comeback attempts on radio and reality television, Clay's foul-mouthed fame proved to be fleeting.

The Adventures of Pluto Nash
(2002, directed by Ron Underwood)

FOR SHEER FINANCIAL CALAMITY, few productions can rival this long-simmering cacophony of a comedy, which cost $120 million to create and brought in a worldwide theatrical gross of $7.1 million.

Set in the year 2080 on the lunar colony of Little America, the film focuses on retired smuggler Pluto Nash (Eddie Murphy), who agrees to buy a nightclub in order to save the venue's owner (Jay Mohr) from being killed by a pair of gangsters. The arrival of a mysterious young woman (Rosario Dawson) who agrees to work at the club to earn money to pay for a trip to Earth sets off a chain of events that brings Pluto and his nightclub posse into a deranged criminal syndicate involved in cloning.

The real meat here, however, is not the film's story. Instead, the flick's backstory is what drives this flop into the anti-classic realm. *The Adventures of Pluto Nash* began its life as a 1985 screenplay and it was the subject of endless rewrites for the next fifteen years before it was ready to go before the camera with Warner Bros. footing an extravagant bill that included an elaborate production design and special effects. Murphy, whose stop-and-start career was in the process of gaining new momentum via imaginative reboots of such old-time films as *The Nutty Professor* (1996) and *Doctor Dolittle* (1998), was brought in as the film's star. But even his presence—along with an all-star cast including Randy Quaid (as an android), John Cleese, Burt Young, Luis Guzman, and an uncredited Alec Baldwin—could not make the vehicle go.

Shot in 2000, Warner Bros. shelved the production in hopes that people would forget about it. For the next two years, whispers of an Eddie Murphy fiasco circulated through Hollywood's gossip channels. The film was unceremoniously dumped into theaters in 2002 without advanced screenings for the critics (most of whom acerbically noted their lack of preview access).

Murphy's career managed to move beyond this disaster, although he unwisely revisited the realm of sci-fi comedy with the 2008 flop *Meet Dave* in which he played a humanoid spaceship for tiny Earth-visiting aliens. *Pluto Nash* director Ron Underwood (best known for helming the 1991 Billy Crystal comedy *City Slickers)* saw his cred diminish substantially—he later found himself directing forgettable cable television movies.

However, the film's box office tailspin managed to attract belated interest among fans of so-bad-they're-good films: a 2003 DVD release stunned many industry experts with nearly $25 million in rental grosses while the Adult Swim channel cult favorite *Robot Chicken* facetiously sought to enshrine the film's place in popular culture by having August 16 (its ignoble theatrical release date) declared a federal holiday by Congress.

Airport 1975
(1974, directed by Jack Smight)

DURING THE EARLY 1970S, a strange genre enjoyed a flurry of excitement: all-star disaster movies in which stellar-packed casts found themselves under assault in natural or manmade catastrophes of extraordinary proportions. Whether the films involved the challenges of surviving in a tidal wave-capsized ocean liner (*The Poseidon Adventure*), outrunning the flames in a burning skyscraper (*The Towering Inferno*), dodging the wreckage and ruin of a collapsing California (*Earthquake*), or riding a doomed Nazi dirigible to its fiery fate (*The Hindenburg*), these films entertained audiences with a surplus of special effects trickery and small armies of stunt doubles handling the dangerous feats that the all-star casts were unable to perform.

Arguably the wackiest entry in this genre was *Airport 1975*, a quasi-sequel to the popular 1970 epic *Airport*, based on Arthur Hailey's bestselling novel. While the original film's climax centered on an airplane that is destroyed in flight by a bomber, the film placed a greater emphasis on various melodramatic storylines rather than the struggle to survive on a damaged airplane.

For *Airport 1975*, a midair collision between a Boeing 747 and a small private plane creates a massive (and aeronautically impossible) hole in the larger aircraft's cockpit, killing two pilots and blinding a third. Although the latter man is able to get the airplane on autopilot, no one on board is able to bring it down for an emergency landing.

Unlike *Airport*, which populated its story with a wealth of compelling characters, *Airport 1975* crams the plot with stock characters whose lack of dimension becomes unintentionally funny. Perhaps the most outrageous characters are a happy, guitar-playing nun (Australian pop star Helen Reddy) and the youthful kidney transplant patient (a post-*Exorcist* Linda Blair) who receives an in-flight serenade from the singing sister. (The 1980 parody *Airplane!* had wicked fun with these inventions.)

And while the other disaster flicks of the era lavished considerable sums on effective special effects, *Airport 1975* was clearly made on the cheap. Universal Pictures originally planned it as a made-for-TV movie and the lack of polish and credible production tricks are too obvious. Although a few notable names were part of the all-star cast, most notably Gloria Swanson (playing herself) and Myrna Loy, the stellar lineup was mostly B-list TV performers: Sid Caesar, Larry Storch, Jerry Stiller, Susan Clark, Norman Fell, Efrem Zimbalist, Jr., Roy Thinnes, Beverly Garland, and a then-unknown Erik Estrada.

The film's leads had cinematic standing: Charlton Heston as a pilot who saves the day through a highly unlikely rescue (I won't spoil the fun on how he achieves this daring feat for those of you who haven't seen it) and Karen Black as the flight attendant who keeps the airplane in motion until Heston's arrival. But both actors were clearly playing with material far below their talents and they were clearly handling their roles with tongue-in-cheek panache. George Kennedy, who was part of the original *Airport* cast, also turned up in a meaningless supporting role.

Back in 1974, audiences accepted any disaster flick that was thrown at them. The commercial success of *Airport 1975* generated two additional sequels, one having an airplane crash into the waters within the Bermuda Triangle and the other involving a bumpy Concorde ride. Needless to say, none of these films would later turn up as in-flight movies.

Alice of Wonderland in Paris
(1966, directed by Gene Deitch)

THE FIRST FEATURE FILM directed by the chronically inept animator Gene Deitch (he was responsible for the creepy and utterly unfunny *Tom and Jerry* and *Popeye* cartoons in the early 1960s), *Alice of Wonderland in Paris* is an absurd offering that jettisons Lewis Carroll and depicts Alice as a bourgeois American girl with a bouffant hairdo, a miniskirt, and an old lady's voice (provided by character actress Norma MacMillan). Alice is already famous (the book *Alice in Wonderland* is spotted on a table), but she is bored—she wants to go to Paris and explore the French capital's hedonistic charms.

"Getting to Wonderland was easy," she rues aloud. "All I had to do was fall down the rabbit hole. But let's face it, it takes money to get to Paris!"

With uncommonly good timing, a talking French mouse named Francois bicycles into Alice's apartment, shrinks her to rodent size, and pedals off with her to Paris. From here, the film conveniently forgets its inane setup and swings into an anthology of short stories, each of which Francois and Alice prefix with a "Let me tell you about…" lead-in.

The short stories presented here include two adventures from the once-popular *Madeline* series of children's books: one has Madeline tolerating Pepito, the boorish son of the Spanish ambassador (he nearly gets killed when his attempt to feed a cat to a pack of dogs goes awry) and the other has Madeline and Pepito running away to join a gypsy circus (when their guardians come searching for them, the gypsies sew the children into a vaudeville lion costume and lock them in a cage—and they like it!). Another story involves Anatole, a Parisian mouse who becomes the vice president of a cheese company.

Also presented is an adaptation of "The Frowning Prince," a bizarre comedy about a young royal who is incapable of smiling, and "Many Moons," based on a charming James Thurber fantasy about a lunar-obsessed princess. In between the stories, Francois takes Alice to a cheese factory and stuffs her with cheese, causing her to turn green.

Even if one could overlook the rickety nature of the screenplay, the animation in *Alice of Wonderland in Paris* damages the viewer with its clumsy and often creepy style. The film looks so shaky that one could imagine the entire production was put together on a lunch break. And forget about the voice performances saving the day: old reliables like Carl Reiner, Howard Morris, and Allen Swift are on the soundtrack, but they couldn't work any magic with the corny and odd dialogue.

Despite being crammed with multiple stories and strange interludes between the talking mouse and the Paris-obsessed Alice, *Alice of Wonderland in Paris* ran a scant fifty-two minutes. On the two occasions when it played in theaters (once in 1966 via Childhood Productions, then in the early 1970s by Paramount Pictures), it was paired with a live-action short film about horses called *White Mane*. In both cases, audiences avoided this unbalanced Alice and her Gallic gang.

All This and World War II
(1976, directed by Susan Winslow)

As part of its year-end cinematic offerings in 1976, 20th Century Fox unleashed something called *All This and World War II*, which combined footage of the Second World War, both documentary newsreel film from the battlefront and glossy Hollywood war movies, and set it against a wall-to-wall music score.

One might think the film's soundtrack would have been reflective of that era, either in the Big Band sounds of Glenn Miller and Harry James or the sophisticated jazz of Duke Ellington and Count Basie. However, the film presents World War II against the music of the Beatles. But not the original Beatles recordings. Instead, a new selection of covers feature the recording stars of the mid-1970s (and a few jokers in the pack).

Starting with the insane imagery of German cavalry galloping into Poland in 1939 while Ambrosia bellows "Roll up for the mystery tour," the film speeds furiously into a weird mix of history and Beatlemania. At first, there is acidic wit on display in the mix-and-match of image and tune: for instance, Peter Gabriel's "Strawberry Fields Forever" warbles how "living is easy with eyes closed" while Neville Chamberlain holds aloft his doomed peace treaty with Germany. Hitler's planning for war at his mountaintop retreat in Berchtesgaden becomes "The Fool on the Hill" as Helen Reddy sings how "the man with the foolish grin is keeping perfectly still."

Things then become increasingly strange: Leo Sayer pours out a Johnnie Ray-worthy crying rendition of "The Long and Winding Road" while Nazi forces push west from Germany through the Lowlands and to the port at Dunkirk. When the Nazi bombing of London reduces wide stretches of the city to fire and rubble, the Bee Gees chime in with "Golden Slumbers." The Pacific conflict is addressed with Tina Turner singing "Come Together" while close-ups of Hirohito and Japanese soldiers are matched to lyrics that tell us "Here comes old flat top" with his "choo choo eyeballs." The Japanese departure for Pearl Harbor has the Bee Gees crooning, "Here comes the Sun King" while the attack itself is scored with Leo Sayer (again?) bellowing, "I am the Walrus."

Adding further confusion to the proceedings is the inclusion of footage from 20th Century Fox war movies. Richard Burton and James Mason enjoy a testy conversation from *The Desert Fox*, which, in turn, sets up a sequence on the Siege of Tobruk scored by the Brothers Johnson singing "Help!" Throughout the film, scenes from *The Longest Day*, *Patton*, *A Bell for Adano*, the Laurel and Hardy comedy *Great Guns*, and *Tora! Tora! Tora!* are dropped in at random. There's even a scene from *Casablanca*, which is interesting since there is no acknowledgment to Warner Bros. for that clip in the closing credits.

Sometimes the film clicks with bizarre surrealism, such as the color footage of the Battle of Midway pegged to Elton John's rendition of "Lucy in the Sky with Diamonds" (which became the only hit single to emerge from the score). Also on target: Mussolini's downfall framed with "Nowhere Man" via Jeff Lynne and the German retreat with Rod Stewart doing "Get Back" while Nazi newsreel footage is run in reverse, showing Hitler and his henchmen marching backward. Stalin sends his Red Army off to the Brothers Johnson singing "Hey Jude" and the D-Day invasion plays alongside Frankie Valli's take on "A Day in the Life."

Yet the film's presentation of the conflict is often curiously antiseptic. New Zealand film critic Shane Burridge noted, "While we get lots of explosions, tanks, and planes, we're spared the body count on the front lines and the horror of the concentration camps."

Upon its release, critics savaged the movie with gusto while audiences (except for rabid Beatles fans) stayed away. The film was yanked quickly from release and the studio hoped the production would be forgotten. Rumors spread that all of the prints of the film were destroyed. However, bootleg copies have found their way into collector-to-collector circulation and the original LP soundtrack (which was never rereleased on compact disc) still turns up on online auction sites.

At Long Last Love
(1975, directed by Peter Bogdanovich)

WHEN DIRECTOR PETER BOGDANOVICH began to establish his reputation in the early 1970s, he made no secret of his taste for nostalgia and it showed in some of his movies. His 1972 romp *What's Up, Doc?* recalled the screwball comedies of the 1930s while his 1973 comedy *Paper Moon* was evocative of the cynical Preston Sturges style of filmmaking. Even his decision to shoot *The Last Picture Show* and *Paper Moon* in black-and-white at a time when all Hollywood productions were in color showed Bogdanovich's desire to stay connected to distant decades.

For *At Long Last Love*, Bogdanovich opted for a return trip to the 1930s, this time to re-create the dream worlds of the Astaire-Rogers musicals. The filmmaker decided to serve up the musical champagne of the era via the Cole Porter songbook and he harvested sixteen songs ranging from classics like "Let's Misbehave" and "I Get a Kick Out of You" to intriguing, lesser-known works like "Most Gentlemen Don't Like Love" and the title song (which was rarely performed owing to an allegedly jinxed history—Porter wrote it to distract himself from excruciating pain while he was awaiting medical help after his legs were crushed in a riding accident).

But Bogdanovich goofed by insisting on live recordings of the musical numbers. It was never quite clear why he wanted to do this—after all, Astaire, Rogers, and their contemporaries were happily lip-syncing their numbers back in the glory days of RKO.

Even more damaging was the decision to put Cybill Shepherd and Burt Reynolds in the leading roles. Neither star was noted for their musical ability, but even if they could sing, they were still badly cast against type. After all, tough guy Reynolds was no one's idea of an effervescent, tuxedo-clad millionaire playboy (Bogdanovich originally toyed with handling the role himself and then tried in vain to convince Elliott Gould to accept the part), while girl-next-door Shepherd could not channel the carefree, Carole Lombard-level of charm to be convincing as a madcap heiress.

The plot of *At Long Last Love* is fairly dumb: millionaire playboy Michael Oliver Pritchard III (Reynolds) is in love with Broadway star Kitty O'Kelly (Madeline Kahn). Heiress Brooke Carter (Shepherd) has the hots for card shark Johnny Spanish (Duilio Del Prete). After dual madcap romances, the couples realize they are mismatched and they change partners. Simultaneously, Brooke's maid (Eileen Brennan) has the hots for Michael's valet (John Hillerman) and wildly pursues him.

All of this involves near-constant singing and dancing at various parties, outings, shopping sprees, and during bathroom hygiene applications. And that is about it. The film is plotless, foolish, and only exists to bridge one musical number to the next.

The resulting critical and commercial backlash was so intense that Bogdanovich took out an advertisement in *The Hollywood Reporter* to offer a halfhearted apology for making the film. Even the unflappable Reynolds (who was no stranger to making bad movies) publicly observed: "I think we bombed."

Atoll K
(1951, directed by Léo Joannon with uncredited co-direction by John Berry)

BY THE LATE 1940S, the comedy team of Stan Laurel and Oliver Hardy were considered has-beens in the U.S. entertainment industry—following the release of their 1945 feature *The Bullfighters*, no employment offers came from Hollywood. However, postwar European audiences still revered the team and their continued popularity on the continent inspired a French-Italian consortium to finance a feature film that would be shot in France.

The resulting production was plagued from start to finish—and beyond—with endless problems. Director Léo Joannon spoke very little English and Laurel and Hardy did not speak French, yet they communicated in the universal language of disagreements. Relations between the director and his stars became so frayed that U.S. director John Berry, who arrived in France after the McCarthy-era blacklist ended his Hollywood career, was quietly brought in to co-direct. Laurel also engaged Alfred J. Goulding and Monte Collins, two of his collaborators from his prime film years, to rework the script.

But production was further delayed when Laurel and Hardy had substantial health problems: Laurel was twice hospitalized, once for prostate surgery and later for dysentery, while Hardy's heart problems added to the state of angst. The production, which was slated for 12 weeks, dragged on for 12 months.

The resulting film was a bizarre libertarian political satire that berated Western governments for excessive taxes and the arms race. Laurel and Hardy, along with a nightclub singer (the lovely Suzy Delair) and two mangy malcontents, somehow find themselves in possession of an island that they call Crusoeland, where they create a constitution which bans taxes and laws. Their little island utopia is thrown into havoc when uranium is discovered, creating a mad power scramble that nearly results in Laurel and Hardy being lynched.

The weird mix of political satire (not exactly Laurel and Hardy's strong points) along with lame slapstick (for which the ill and aging comics struggled gamely) was a comic disaster. Rarely had comedians of a legendary status ever been stuck with such badly conceived material; the sheer strangeness of this endeavor made it fascinating to watch, albeit in a train wreck-viewing sort of way.

The sorry film limped around foreign markets for years under a number of titles, premiering in France as *Atoll K* in 1951 before heading to Great Britain as *Robinson Crusoeland* in 1952. No major U.S. distributor would touch the film, which left the tiny Philadelphia-based Exploitation Pictures to acquire it in 1954 and dump it (minus eighteen minutes of its original running time) in American theaters in a scattershot release under the wishful title *Utopia*.

In the ultimate cruel joke, the truncated *Utopia* was never registered for a copyright. As a result, it has been the subject of excessive duping by cheapo public domain labels, making Laurel and Hardy's least characteristic film their most widely seen in home entertainment release.

The Babe Ruth Story
(1948, directed by Roy Del Ruth)

WILLIAM BENDIX, a burly character actor who earned a niche playing mild villains and decent bumblers, had a rare opportunity to enjoy a starring role as the legendary George Herman "Babe" Ruth. However, Bendix was asked to depict Ruth in a manner that mirrored one of his most prominent roles—the good-natured, yet oafish Chester Riley on the radio series *The Life of Riley.*

As a result, Ruth becomes a childlike character with an unusual penchant for aiding children. This is taken to an outlandish extreme in the notorious "called shot" sequence when Ruth promises to hit a home run for a dying boy during the 1932 World Series. The child's family, listening at home by the radio with the boy lying on his deathbed, reacts to the news of the home run with the same enthusiasm that must have been shared in Jerusalem when the word spread of Jesus' empty tomb. And in true biblical fashion, the radio announcement causes the dying boy to open his eyes slowly and grin widely as his family embraces his now-healthy body with manic love.

This candy-coated fantasy carefully avoids the more intriguing aspects of Ruth's life. The slugger's fondness for fast living, his first marriage to Helen Woodford, and his daughter, Dorothy (whose mother was Ruth's mistress, Juanita Jennings), were nowhere to be found on-screen. But their absence was compensated by a surplus of jolly anachronisms, most notably with the presence of a beer advertisement on a billboard positioned in a stadium game that occurred during the Prohibition years.

Ruth was in poor health at the time of the film's production, which makes the ending overly optimistic with the ailing baseball great (his throat cancer is not identified in the film) agreeing to receive a mysterious experimental serum. The *New York Times* reacted negatively to the sequence, complaining that it was a "tedious and tasteless sick-bed ordeal, with soundtrack sobs and angel voices."

The Babe Ruth Story became a laughingstock in the sports film genre and critic Hal Erickson wasn't off base when he dubbed this production the "*Plan 9 From Outer Space* of baseball biopics." Amazingly, Bendix was called back to the diamond two years later for another starring role in the 1950 comedy *Kill the Umpire*.

Battlefield Earth
(2000, directed by Roger Christian)

L. RON HUBBARD OCCUPIES a bizarre perch in American culture based on his twin careers as a science fiction writer and a do-it-yourself theologian. As a writer, Hubbard's work was adequate, though hardly memorable. In terms of theology, however, Hubbard had far greater prominence through his efforts to create and launch the Church of Scientology.

Over the years, public wariness of the cult aspects of Scientology abated somewhat as several prominent celebrities publicly affirmed their allegiance to the religion. One of the most notable is John Travolta, who sought to adapt Hubbard's sprawling novel *Battlefield Earth* as a two-part epic. While the Hollywood studios were apprehensive about being associated with anything related to Hubbard, the independent American production company Franchise Pictures and the German Intertainment AG stepped in to assist the production.

Set in the year 3000, *Battlefield Earth* is a slave revolt story that pits the remnants of the human race against the alien Psychlos, a bizarre species that have oversized heads crowned with dreadlocks and round bodies with exaggerated groins. The Psychlo security chief (played by Travolta) entrusts a human slave (Barry Pepper) with a Psychlo-level education that would enable him to coordinate an illicit gold mining operation in a radioactive area. Of course, the newly-educated slave uses his Psychlo smarts to lead a revolution to bring down the alien reign of terror.

Despite a $44 million dollar budget (of which $5 million came from Travolta's personal fortune), *Battlefield Earth* emerged as a visually amateurish experience. The bizarre Psychlo makeup, director Roger Christian's insistence on shooting a surplus number of scenes with tilted angles and intrusive color tinting, and a claptrap story mixed with dozens of well-worn adventure story clichés resulted in an unwatchable experience. Critics went out of their way to insult the film—the *Washington Post*'s Rita Kempley insisted that "a million monkeys with a million crayons would be hard-pressed in a million years to create anything as cretinous as *Battlefield Earth*," while Roger Ebert predicted that it would become a "film that for decades to come will be the punch line of jokes about bad movies."

Travolta would later respond to the harsh reviews by stating, "I'd rather my films connect with audiences than with critics because it gives you more longevity as a performer." However, that connection never happened. *Battlefield Earth* crashed at the box office and the envisioned second part of the epic was never made.

But there was a sequel of sorts: Intertainment AG sued Franchise Pictures, claiming that the U.S. company submitted "grossly fraudulent and inflated budgets" that erroneously gave the impression of a $75 million production. In 2004, a court awarded Intertainment AG $121.7 million in damages.

Beat the Devil
(1954, directed by John Huston)

A CRITICAL AND COMMERCIAL FLOP in its day, this aggressively offbeat production has since been embraced with surprising vigor from some cinematic thought leaders, most notably Dave Kehr (who called the movie "the birthplace of camp"). Or perhaps the belated appreciation is just a case of wishful thinking due to the significant talent involved here.

Beat the Devil takes place in a dingy Italian port where a group of travelers wait for a leaky East Africa-bound boat to be fixed. This collection includes a variety of petty crooks, shady characters, and kooks and all of them seem to be heading to Africa in search of uranium deposits. Key to this adventure is an American mercenary (Humphrey Bogart), who brings his Italian wife (Gina Lollobrigida) along for this work. There is also a British couple awaiting passage and the blond wife (Jennifer Jones) seems to have a fancy for the Yank gun-for-hire. A criminal ring that includes Robert Morley and Peter Lorre joins the voyage and everyone becomes caught in a political uprising when they disembark in Africa.

Huston reportedly threw out the original script to *Beat the Devil* at the start of production and flew in Truman Capote to the Italian location to rewrite the movie on a day-by-day basis. No one, perhaps not even Capote, knew where the film was heading, which resulted in a meandering production with scenes that dribble and hobble along without actually achieving a sense of purpose.

The ragged, improvised nature of *Beat the Devil* confused those involved in the production, most notably Bogart, who was also the producer and chief financier of the film. Outside of financial and emotional pains from the production, Bogart also wound up with physical aches: his teeth and tongue were injured in a car accident. As he healed, a then-unknown Peter Sellers was hired to dub some of his lines—to this day, no one can tell which lines came from Sellers's uncanny imitation.

Adding to the confusion was Huston's decision to cast Lollobrigida in her first English-language movie, which was a problem since she didn't speak a word of English and needed to learn her lines phonetically.

United Artists picked up the film for U.S. release due solely to its star power, but the company promoted it as an action film—a major mistake considering there was very little genuine action. The *New York Times* led the brickbats by sneering how "the fun wears mighty thin" and mentioning "the film's harsh, neo-realistic photography, which authentically stalks and X-rays the joke to death."

Years later, apologist critics would rediscover the film and try to convince audiences that it was something of value. Don't you believe it!

Beyond the Sea
(2004, directed by Kevin Spacey)

THE KEY ATTRACTION to *Beyond the Sea* is the bizarre spectacle of a forty-five-year-old Kevin Spacey trying to be something he is not: Bobby Darin when he was a youthful pop star in the late 1950s and early 1960s. Yes, Darin was a versatile star with a tumultuous life, but he died at the age of thirty-seven and any biopic on his meteoric rise to fame required someone closer in age.

Despite wearing blatantly obvious toupees and the heaviest makeup this side of a kabuki theater, Spacey is totally unable to capture the illusion of youth. This is especially painful in his love scenes with Kate Bosworth, who plays Darin's wife Sandra Dee. Spacey and Bosworth look like father and daughter rather than youthful peers and it throws the whole love story subplot badly out of whack.

The problem is further compounded by Spacey's insistence on performing Darin's songs himself rather than lip-sync to his classic recordings. As a singer, Spacey does a wonderful imitation of Jerry Vale, but his warbling bears little resemblance to Darin's distinctive vocalizing.

It actually gets worse. Borrowing a notion from the Dennis Potter bag of tricks, *Beyond the Sea* inserts musical fantasy sequences into the midst of an otherwise straightforward dramatic biopic. Thus, people start to dance in the streets and up staircases without provocation or purpose—this is not a musical, but a music-enhanced shock to the senses. This may have been acceptable if Spacey could dance. But, as you probably guessed, the star failed here, too. As a dancer, Spacey lumbers about like a tranquilized horse fighting to stay awake. It is amusing for all the wrong reasons.

Who's to blame for this madness? We could point to the director, who is none other than Kevin Spacey. Or to the misguided screenwriters, one of which is Kevin Spacey. Or to producers who assembled this mess, one of which is Kevin Spacey.

Mick LaSalle of the *San Francisco Chronicle* pretty much nailed it when he called the endeavor "jaw-droppingly awful, a misbegotten and ill-conceived vanity project." Stephen Holden of the *New York Times* was more succinct, dismissing the film as "a mess." Audiences avoided the flick and the resulting box office flop helped to significantly diminish Spacey's cred as a leading man. Ultimately, the misguided star should have dropped this project beyond the sea and stuck to playing people his own age.

The Bible: In the Beginning
(1966, directed by John Huston)

THIS GRAND ENDEAVOR was among the seemingly endless number of multinational epic collaborations that polluted cinemas during the 1960s. It was helmed by an Italian producer (Dino De Laurentiis) and an American director (John Huston) who brought together a mix of U.S. and European actors and a Japanese composer (Toshirô Mayuzumi) to recreate the first twenty-two chapters of the book of Genesis in the glories of a widescreen process called Dimension 150. Alas, the result was a vulgar and bewildering disaster that earned derision from faithful and agnostics alike.

The main problem was that the film had no cohesive style. The segments ranged from excessively artsy (the Creation and Adam and Eve) to anvil melodrama (Cain and Abel) to light comedy (Noah and the Flood) to spectacle (the Tower of Babel) to soap opera (Abraham and Sarah) to just plain weird (Sodom and Gomorrah with Peter O'Toole playing all three of the angels) to a dreary fizzle (Abraham and Isaac).

Huston cast himself as the voice of God, but was then forced to also take on the role of Noah when he was unable to persuade either Charlie Chaplin or Alec Guinness to play the part. Ironically, Huston was also the second choice to direct the film—he arrived only because De Laurentiis was unable to secure Orson Welles as director. (Robert Bresson was briefly attached to the project, but was dismissed over a dispute on filming the animals in the Noah sequence.)

Despite a wealth of glittery stars hired to keep viewers distracted (George C. Scott and Ava Gardner as Abraham and Sarah, Stephen Boyd as Babel's Nimrod, a pre-*Camelot* Richard Harris and Franco Nero as Cain and Abel, and unclothed hotties Michael Parks and Ulla Bergryd as Adam and Eve), the resulting production moved at a funereal pace that flattened the solemnity of the source material into a dreary wreck. The sweep and scope of the biblical stories never permeated Huston's film; yes, it was all quite eye-catching, but the emotional depth (let alone maturity) of the Old Testament was absent from the screen.

Bosley Crowther, reviewing the film for the *New York Times*, hit upon the film's strengths and weaknesses: "For all its size, for all its extravagant production, its extraordinary special effects, its stunning projection on the wide screen (D-150) and its almost three-hour length, *The Bible* is lacking a sense of conviction of God in so much magnitude or a galvanizing feeling of connection in the stories from Genesis."

De Laurentiis originally planned to use this film to launch a continuous series of Bible-inspired films. The commercial failure of this endeavor encouraged him to switch gears and focus on producing films such as *Danger: Diabolik*, *Barbarella*, the 1976 *King Kong* remake, and other films of a significantly non-sacred nature.

Birdemic: Shock and Terror
(2010, directed by James Nguyen)

JUST WHEN YOU THOUGHT it was safe to go back to the theater, along comes James Nguyen's *Birdemic: Shock and Terror*—a $10,000 rip-off of Alfred Hitchcock's classic *The Birds*. Indeed, you've never truly experienced bad filmmaking until you've seen this.

What's wrong here? Well, the special effects are among the most atrocious ever put on camera: stuffed birds hanging in midair with unmoving wings and animation that appears to have been created with DOS software.

But at least some sort of effort went into creating those shabby effects—at least the birds didn't fall off their wires. The rest of the film, however, shows no signs whatsoever of any professional considerations: the sound recording is haphazard, the cinematography is often poorly lit, the music score is repetitive and monotonous, the screenplay is a weird collection of illogical dialogue and contrived scenes, and no one on camera knows how to act (although romantic leads Alan Bagh and Whitney Moore are fairly good-looking, which might be the film's sole saving grace).

Indeed, the closest thing to genuine talent found here is, of all people, Tippi Hedren. Yes, Hitchcock's last great blonde is linked to this madness, albeit as a cheat. She is seen in a clip from an earlier Nguyen film in which she had a brief appearance.

Nguyen's sloppiness permeated to his promotional efforts. His attempt to market the film at the 2009 Sundance Film Festival resulted in error-riddled materials that misspelled the film's website as "Bidemic.com" and a tagline that asked "Why Did the Eagles and Vultures Attacked?"

Incredibly, a respected distributor (Severin Films) picked up the film for release and secured theatrical bookings (mostly as a midnight movie) in the United States and Canada. Overheated reviews that emphasized its incompetence—*The Village Voice* said it belonged in "the pantheon of beloved trash-terpieces"—only helped pique interest in the production. As a result, audiences eager for a so-bad-it's-good turkey got to feast on Nguyen's wacky birds.

And, of course, the film wound up generating a sequel: *Birdemic II: The Resurrection*. Indeed, H. L. Mencken was right—n*obody ever went broke underestimating the taste of the American public*!

The Black Cauldron
(1985, directed by Ted Berman and Richard Rich)

BACK IN 1985, Walt Disney Pictures had very high hopes for *The Black Cauldron*. It was the studio's twenty-fifth animated feature, its first PG-rated animated film, and its most expensive animated endeavor to date ($25 million). It included the studio's first use of computer-generated animation and it was the first time since 1959's *Sleeping Beauty* that an animated feature was shot in 70mm.

Today, however, the film is mostly remembered as being one of the studio's biggest flops.

What went wrong? For starters, the source material—*The Chronicles of Prydain* book series by Lloyd Alexander—clearly baffled the studio in its attempts to turn the five-volume literary series into a family-friendly film running under ninety minutes. Nine writers were credited in turning out the screenplay, which flip-flopped between surrealism and connect-the-dots action. Unwilling to take a chance on a genuinely mature work, but unable to let go of the kid-friendly Disney style, the resulting production came across like second-rate Tolkien work with the genuinely scary parts filtered out.

Set in medieval times, the film follows the unlikely evolution of headstrong young Taran from a rural assistant pig-keeper to a bold warrior fighting to stop the Horned King from gaining control of the darkly magical black cauldron. The film is peppered with several stereotypical stock characters, including a spunky princess and two bumbling sidekicks (an inept elderly minstrel and a furry creature with a Donald Duck voice).

However, the film has a surprise element: a psychic pig plays a key role in the plot. Sadly, the pig has no dialogue. Indeed, unlike other Disney romps, there are no talking animals—and no songs, which is a shame since musical interludes could have added some oxygen to this gaseous mess.

For all of the money that went into the film, it is somewhat peculiar that the animation is so clumsy. Even the film's supposed centerpiece, the skeletal-faced Horned King, looks like he wandered in from a *Scooby-Doo* mystery.

In fairness, *The Black Cauldron* has one genuinely funny moment, albeit in the form of a cheap laugh: the old minstrel gets turned into a frog and stuck in the deep cleavage of a zaftig witch. But don't expect that magical moment to be turned into a Disney World attraction!

Disney realized it had a problem with this production. Studio chairman Jeffrey Katzenberg, who was relatively new to the company at the time, ordered the deletion of several scenes due to concerns over their graphic nature. When producer Joe Hale balked at the order, Katzenberg himself brought the film into an edit bay and physically excised the offensive material. The film would have to undergo additional cuts in order to satisfy the Motion Picture Association of America's standards for a PG rating.

Ultimately, it didn't help. Despite a surprisingly high number of positive reviews, audiences were cold to this strange and unusual endeavor. The film was among the rare money-losing Disney animated features and for years, the studio kept it out of circulation. *The Black Cauldron* finally emerged again on VHS in 1998, then in DVD versions released in 2000 and 2010.

Black Devil Doll From Hell
(1984, directed by Chester Novell Turner)

THIS NO-BUDGET, shot-on-video oddity combines the Zuni doll segment of the classic TV movie *Trilogy of Terror* with the ventriloquist's dummy chapter of the British horror masterpiece *Dead of Night* and then mixes them into a blaxploitation setting. In this film, religious fanatic Helen Black (played by atonal nonprofessional Shirley L. Jones) finds herself alone in an amoral world. She chastises a jive-talking petty thief who sells stolen merchandise from the trunk of his car and later berates a friend who tries to set her up on a date. "I'm not interested in Sam," she says about her would-be Lothario. "All he wants to do is get between my legs."

One day, Helen goes to a schlocky gift store run by a tiny woman who appears to be wearing Butterfly McQueen's costume from *Gone with the Wind*. Helen spies a black ventriloquist's dummy with a head full of dreadlocks. Although the store's owner warns her that the dummy has a strange history—it somehow found its way back to the property after being sold on four separate occasions—Helen thinks it would be a cute addition to her house full of religious bric-a-brac.

That night, Helen begins having nightmares that the doll is having sex with her. At one point in her ghastly dreams, she is running through her home while the doll rides on her, piggyback-style. However, upon waking, Helen finds herself in an even worse nightmare—the doll has come alive and is eager to take sexual advantage of her. "Wake up, bitch!" the doll growls at the sleeping Helen.

And how does Helen react to being sexually assaulted by a ventriloquist's dummy? Well, it seems like she loves it to the point that she quickly jettisons her Bible-thumping ways and becomes the newest slut in the 'hood. And although the local studs are fun to have around, Helen realizes that her doll has (pardon the pun) the best wood around.

Black Devil Doll From Hell was the creation of one Chester Novell Turner, whose only other confirmed feature film is a 1987 obscurity called *Tales from the Quadead Zone*. Biographical material on Turner is scant—the Internet Movie Database (IMDb) claims he was born in 1950 and SoiledSinema.com says that he died in a car crash in 1996, but beyond those factoids, the filmmaker remains an elusive mystery.

However, it is safe to assume that Turner had no filmmaking education whatsoever. *Black Devil Doll From Hell* launches with an interminable opening credits sequence that runs an astonishing six minutes, which is then capped by thirty seconds of blank screen. The production appears to have been shot on some crummy camcorder and the sound is frequently unintelligible. A synthesizer music score is dropped helter-skelter throughout the soundtrack, often muffling the dialogue.

As for the puppet—well, despite a Redd Foxx-style gravelly voice and a scatological vocabulary, this doll is the least threatening creature in horror movie history. The doll is operated with such incompetence that the only reaction it could possibly generate is laughter. Indeed, the rape sequence—which includes having the doll's Popsicle-stick tongue licking Jones's breasts—is so ridiculous that it steamrolls the underlying misogynist theme into unadulterated camp.

Although the film has a mild cult following, not everyone is enthused with this production. Steven Puchalski, editor and publisher of *Shock Cinema* magazine, says of this production: "I can't imagine an uglier, more unbelievably inept piece of rotgut." Michael Musto of *The Village Voice* said it was the worst film ever made, adding it was "unbearable, offensive… the whole thing looks like it cost less than two cents and a blow job."

The Blue Bird
(1976, directed by George Cukor)

THE BLUE BIRD was the first and only American-Soviet motion picture coproduction, created in the spirit of fostering better relations between the rival Cold War superpowers, but doomed by the forces of stupidity and incompetence. If the Americans and the Soviets couldn't work together on a movie, did anyone genuinely believe they could work together for the cause of world peace?

Emboldened by President Richard Nixon's attempts to foster better relationships between the Cold War rivals, the powers of 20th Century Fox engaged the chieftains of the Soviet film industry to join forces in a collaborative effort. Unfortunately, it took three years of painfully protracted negotiations before the two sides could even agree on the subject of their joint venture, which turned out to be Maurice Maeterlinck's classic children's theater piece *The Blue Bird*. The choice seemed like a wise one since the decidedly nonpolitical play was well-loved by Russian audiences while 20th Century Fox already owned the rights to the property, having previously made a version of it in 1940 starring Shirley Temple.

The new production was shot in the Soviet Union with George Cukor (of all people) as director and Elizabeth Taylor starring in four different roles. At this point in time, Taylor was having quite a battle with her weight and the overtaxed costume designers were hard-pressed to shoehorn the zaftig diva into outfits that would not betray her excess poundage. Cukor grandly helped the star by posing the film's two young child actors in front of her as often as possible as if to hide the scale-tipping superstar from full audience scrutiny.

The Blue Bird involves the adventures of two peasant children who fall asleep in a forest and somehow share a simultaneous dream about their search for the Blue Bird of Happiness (yes, that's where the expression came from). In this dreamland, a variety of animals, objects, and concepts receive anthropomorphic life. This means we are treated to the sight of people dressed up as a dog, a cat, a loaf of bread, a flame, a bowl of sugar, and as light and night. Elizabeth Taylor is the Queen of Light (complete with tiara and tacky magic wand) while Jane Fonda (wearing a black leather outfit strangely similar to the Darth Vader costume) is the Night. Also rounding out the cast is Ava Gardner as Luxury, Robert Morley as Father Time (he even got to carry a huge hourglass), and Cicely Tyson as the cat. Soviet actors took up most of the remaining roles.

The production was bedeviled by endless delays, the difficulty in merging American and Soviet work ethics, and health issues involving Taylor and comic actor James Coco, who was originally cast as the dog, but developed gall bladder problems during production and was forced to leave halfway through; his scenes were reshot with George Cole in the canine costume.

The resulting effort was a gooey bit of muck that played like a third-rate rip-off of *The Wizard of Oz*. Americans mostly ignored the final film while the Kremlin banned the film for years.

Boys Beware
(1961, directed by Sid Davis)

TOO OFTEN, the only thing you can learn from educational movies is how not to make movies. Seriously, the films are sticky and sentimental with their anvil messages, they require kids to become slavishly obedient to adult authority and not question the wisdom of grown-ups, or they are just plain weird. And on occasion, an educational film teaches subjects in a thoroughly incorrect and atrocious manner.

One of the most notoriously awful educational films of all time is a ten-minute monstrosity from 1961 called *Boys Beware*. What should boys beware of? Well, if this film is to be believed, boys should be afraid of homosexuals. And why should boys be afraid of homosexuals? Because, according to this educational film, homosexuals exist to sexually molest and murder clean-cut youths. Yes, *Boys Beware* provides gays with the same positive image that *The Birth of a Nation* offered African-Americans.

Allegedly produced in accordance with the police departments and school board of Inglewood, California, *Boys Beware* is narrated by one Lieutenant Williams of the "juvenile division" of the local police house. He offers a wealth of stories of young lads who were seduced and ruined by big, bad homos.

The first story revolves around Jimmy Barnes, who gets involved with a lascivious older man he met one afternoon while hitchhiking. The next involves young Mike Merritt (you may notice that no one in educational film has ethnic names—only WASP kids get into trouble here). Mike is a teen who gets the attention of a seemingly harmless older guy at a basketball court. The older man offers to drive Mike home. Bad idea, Mike!

Then we have two more quickie vignettes: a newspaper delivery boy gets into a car with a stranger, but one of the kid's pals gets the license plate number. Hooray for the motorcycle cops, who arrive to save the day and the kid before the dreadful queer gets his fly down. There is also a mini-tale of potential problems at a public restroom, but the quick-thinking kid makes a Road Runner-worthy getaway from the evil queen at the urinals.

Lieutenant Williams tells his audience to be very, very afraid: "One never knows when a homosexual is about. He may appear normal and it may be too late when you discover he is mentally ill."

Made for a thousand dollars, *Boys Beware* is played entirely in pantomime while Lieutenant Williams's incessant narration explains what is taking place. The low budget also affected the vehicular props: Williams and all of the lascivious predators drive the exact same car! Filmmaker Sid Davis cast himself as the predatory miscreant in the restroom—hey, if Hitchcock could make cameos in his movies, why couldn't Sid Davis?

Bubble
(2005, directed by Steven Soderbergh)

STEVEN SODERBERGH, the Oscar-winning filmmaker who has carved out a lucrative Hollywood niche directing star vehicles for the likes of Julia Roberts and George Clooney, unwisely ignored Thomas Wolfe's axiom and tried to go home again—in his case, to his low-budget indie film roots. The result of this mistake was *Bubble*, which is arguably the director's worst film.

Bubble takes place in a doll factory located in a small town along the economically depressed Ohio-West Virginia border region. Two of the employees of this factory are Martha (a short, fat, middle-aged woman who lives with her feeble old father) and Kyle (a tall, thin, young man who lives with his mother in a trailer). Martha gushes that Kyle is her best friend, but he never openly repays that compliment. Their friendship is disrupted when the factory hires Rose, who is the polar opposite of Martha. She is young, thin, pretty, smokes cigarettes, and is sexually active. (She has a two-year-old daughter, even though she's not married.)

Things come to a head when Rose asks Martha to babysit her daughter. Martha agrees only to learn too late that the reason for this is so that Rose can go on a date with Kyle. The next morning, Rose is found dead in her home. While logic might suggest the culprit is Rose's ex-boyfriend (who stalked Rose during her date and made a very loud scene after Kyle went home), Martha isn't entirely free of police suspicion.

With *Bubble*, Soderbergh made the fatal mistake of casting the main roles with nonprofessional actors who lived in the region where the film is set. None of these people had previous acting experience; in real life, Martha is played by a KFC manager, Kyle is a computer student, and Rose is a hair stylist. In reel life, however, this stab at hillbilly neo-realism fails because none of these people have any talent. The performances are so stiff and embarrassing that *Bubble* is an HD endurance test—George A. Romero's zombies have more life, style, and soul than the leading players here.

Incredibly, even worse performances come from the local police, who play themselves on-screen. These cops may not think twice about jumping into dangerous situations when busting criminals, but they are so visibly nervous when reciting their lines that one cannot help but feel pity for them.

Bubble also had one of the worst musical scores ever put in a movie: an annoying, fumbling guitar score which sounds more like a string being tuned than a genuine score.

Bubble was the first in a proposed series of cheap indies to be lensed in HD in various locations across America. That series pretty much popped with the critical and commercial failure of *Bubble* and Soderbergh has (thankfully) not made the same mistake twice.

The Buster Keaton Story
(1957, directed by Sidney Sheldon)

COMPARED TO THIS FEATURE, the previously discussed production *The Babe Ruth Story* is a documentary of frightening accuracy. The rise and fall of the great silent comedy star was certainly a compelling story, but almost nothing of that tumultuous existence finds its way into this offering.

In this bizarre fantasy, Keaton is the son of struggling vaudeville performers who sneaks into "Famous Studios" and catches the eye of casting director Gloria Brent, who successfully convinces the studio head to sign the acrobatic lad. Initially hired as a bit player, he quickly becomes a star and director. He becomes smitten with leading lady Peggy Courtney, but her lack of interest in him causes him to begin drinking heavily. His big silent comedy *The Gambler* opens the same day as *The Jazz Singer* and flops and Keaton's attempt to adapt to talking pictures is wrecked by a caustic director. Considered an alcoholic has-been, he is reunited with Gloria, who marries him and joins him on a vaudeville tour. And when Gloria reveals she is pregnant, they prepare for a new act called "The Three Keatons."

Even if one could ignore the gross fabrications of this story—there was no "Famous Studios," Keaton was married three times, there was no such film called *The Gambler,* and the problems Keaton experienced in the transition to sound had nothing to do with his alleged incompetence in handling dialogue—it is still impossible to overlook the idea that happy-go-lucky song-and-dance man Donald O'Connor was both physically and emotionally wrong for the title role. O'Connor reportedly studied Keaton's silent comedies at great length, but obviously learned nothing from the experience. His attempts to duplicate The Great Stone Face's pratfalls and physical feats were pathetic.

Keaton, who was paid fifty thousand by Paramount Pictures for the rights to his life story, was so aghast at the film that he reportedly tried to leave the theater when this mess was being premiered. To his credit, he never publicly complained about the film: the money he gained from selling his story was used to purchase the Woodland Hills, California, home where he lived with his third wife, Eleanor, until his death in 1966.

As for Keaton's other wives, first wife Natalie Talmadge (with whom he had two sons) was reportedly an alcoholic recluse at the time of the film's release and it is unknown whether she ever saw the film. Second wife Mae Scriven (a nurse who was briefly married to Keaton during the period of his most precarious alcoholism) saw the film and filed a $5 million lawsuit against Paramount Pictures, which is interesting considering that no character in the film bore any resemblance to her. It is unclear how the case was settled, though one could imagine the bickering among the various attorneys was more entertaining than this film.

Butterfly
(1982, directed by Matt Cimber)

IN 1982, the Hollywood Foreign Press Association (HFPA) received a wave of hostile criticism when it presented its Golden Globe for Best Female Newcomer to the little-known Pia Zadora for her performance in the barely seen independent production *Butterfly*. The problem, it turned out, was that Zadora's husband, Israeli hotel mogul Meshulam Riklis, who financed *Butterfly*, flew HFPA members to Las Vegas on an extravagant junket as part of a blatant lobbying effort to secure award status for his wife. The HFPA, embarrassed by this revelation, discontinued its newcomer award the following year.

While most people recall that Golden Globes scandal, few recall the film at the center of the brouhaha. Adapted from a half-forgotten novel by James M. Cain, *Butterfly* provides a weird mix of incest, revenge, greed, and long-simmering family feuds. Zadora plays Kady, the estranged, slutty daughter of a hermit (Stacy Keach), who lives in the Nevada desert and guards an abandoned silver mine. The father-and-daughter reunion is complicated when other characters—a second long-lost daughter who brings along Kady's illegitimate child, Kady's ex-boyfriend (who is also the child's father), the hermit's ex-wife, and the man who seduced the hermit's ex-wife into leaving him so many years ago—enter the story. Needless to say, things get a little crowded and convoluted for the poor old hermit.

Riklis's money enabled *Butterfly* to be packed with fading film stars (Lois Nettleton, Edward Albert, James Franciscus, Stuart Whitman) and a couple of unexpected surprises, including Ed McMahon (in a rare dramatic film role) and Orson Welles (as a lecherous judge in a bit part that somehow snagged him a Golden Globe Award nomination as Best Supporting Actor).

As for Zadora, her attempts to play the role of a brazen sexpot created a wealth of unintended laughs. She lacked the raw, visceral emotional power that the role required and instead came across like a kid trying to be Mae West. Her performance earned her two Razzies—for Worst New Star and Worst Actress—and her attempts to be taken seriously as a film performer were immediately doomed after her Golden Globe became tarnished. After a few barely seen B-level productions, including *Fake-Out* (1982), *The Lonely Lady* (1983), and *Voyage of the Rock Aliens* (1985), Zadora abruptly withdrew from trying to become a film superstar.

In a way, Zadora was the victim of the ages-old problem of trying to push a talent into a mold that did not suit that individual's abilities and personality. Her amusing cameo roles in John Waters's *Hairspray* (1988) and in *Naked Gun 33⅓: The Final Insult* (1994) presented a gift for light comedy that was absent from *Butterfly* and her other films. In the years since then, she has also proven herself to be a talented pop singer with a number of well-received albums and concert tours to her credit. Perhaps if she had the right vehicle back in 1982, she might have become a major Hollywood presence. Oh well, that's showbiz!

Can Heironymus Merkin Ever Forget Mercy Humppe and Find True Happiness?
(1969, directed by Anthony Newley)

CLEARLY INSPIRED BY Fellini's *8½*, *Heironymus Merkin* is a surreal emotionalinventory check of a burned-out creative artist taking stock of his unusual life. But whereas Fellini masterfully mixed surreal imagery with inspired madness, director/writer/star Anthony Newley runs amok with smutty gags, obscure humor, terrible songs, and a sense of overstuffed self-importance. The audience doesn't watch this film; instead, the film's shameless explosions of bad taste and bad sense assault the audience.

Newley's Heironymus Merkin is a just-turned-forty performer who is building a museum to himself. The film opens along the seashore as Merkin addresses an audience consisting of his mother and his daughters, Thumbelina and Thaxted (Newley's real-life kids), regarding his plans. He then unfolds his own life story through a series of stories that may or may not be true. The most outlandish of these tales finds Merkin (dressed like a marionette, complete with strings and white face makeup) learning the act of entertainment from Uncle Limelight, a music hall performer played by veteran British funnyman Bruce Forsyth. Uncle Limelight's trademark song is "Picadilly Lilly" and Forsyth goes to town with a no-holds-barred, knockout performance that could've earned him an Oscar nomination if the sequence was part of a better film. Sadly, Newley keeps interrupting Forsyth's work with irrelevant shots of himself squealing and clapping like a happy marionette being manipulated by an off-screen puppeteer.

The rest of the film is a mind-boggling hodgepodge relating to Merkin's ascent to manhood, his discovery and expertise at sex, and his career trajectory as managed by one Goodtime Eddie Filth, a devil in disguise played by a clearly embarrassed Milton Berle. Haunting Merkin throughout the film is a man in a white suit known as The Presence, who is played by the ancient comic George Jessel. This character spits out creaky jokes that have nothing to do with the film, but they are weirdly funny as surreal interruptions.

Every now and then, the action is interrupted by a group of producers and writers in a movie sound studio who are constantly complaining about the story's lack of coherence. If you look closely, you can find veteran comic Stubby Kaye in the mix, but he is given nothing funny to say.

As a love letter to himself, Newley gives new meaning to the concept of vanity. In the course of the film, he beds the likes of the eponymous Mercy Humppe, the charming Filigree Fondle, the dramatic Trampolena Whambang (with whom he stages a naughty show called *The Princess and the Donkey*), and the sultry Polyester Poontang. The last woman is played by Joan Collins, Newley's then-wife, who looks stunning, but is forced to sing something called "Chalk and Cheese" while Newley cavorts naked. I am not certain which is worse: Anthony Newley naked or Joan Collins singing.

The resulting film was a critical and commercial disaster and Newley's career never truly recovered from the fiasco; over the years, however, the film managed to snag a small but devoted cult following.

The Cat in the Hat
(2003, directed by Bo Welch)

THIS PRODUCTION first came together in 1997 when Dreamworks acquired the big-screen rights to Dr. Seuss's classic book. Rather than pursue an animated offering along the lines of the celebrated 1971 made-for-television special, it was decided to create a live-action version that incorporated fanciful production design and CGI effects to bring Dr. Seuss's wonderfully warped vision to life.

Although a screenplay was created, producer Brian Glazer put *The Cat in the Hat* on the back burner and pursued another Dr. Seuss classic with his 2000 version of *How the Grinch Stole Christmas*. That film's box office success encouraged Glazer to return to *The Cat in the Hat* as his next Dr. Seuss-inspired work.

At that point, the production became an endless skein of problems. The original screenplay was jettisoned and new writers were hired to bang out a script, but that delay caused the film's original star, Tim Allen, to bow out due to other commitments. Mike Myers was then brought in to play the eponymous feline, but he added his own ideas to the screenplay (and, reportedly, muscled out director Bo Welch in determining how certain sequences should be staged).

Although the film retained the basic framework of the mysterious bipedal feline creating havoc for two young siblings who are home alone on a rainy day, the personality of the resulting film bore very little resemblance to the delightful anarchy of the Dr. Seuss book. Myers's cat engaged in flatulence, Benny Hill-style risqué sight gags, crass double entendres— he refers to a muddy garden tool as a "dirty hoe"—and borderline profanity, including an aborted attempt to spell out the acronym for the Super

Hydraulic Instantaneous Transporter. While Myers's makeup came close to the Dr. Seuss concept of the character, the actor inexplicably made his character sound like Bert Lahr's Cowardly Lion.

In an effort to pad the running time, *The Cat in the Hat* introduced new subplots (including detailed explanations of personality deficiencies for the children visited by the manic feline) and new characters, including Alec Baldwin as an obnoxious neighbor who is infatuated with the children's single mother and Paris Hilton as herself in a party sequence. Needless to say, these embellishments made a bad situation worse.

Reviews for *The Cat in the Hat* were overwhelmingly negative. The *Seattle Post-Intelligencer*'s William Arnold condemned it as "ugly, dumb, and colossally mean-spirited" while *The A.V. Club*'s Nathan Rabin called it a "clattering abomination." The film received eight Razzie Award nominations, winning the prize for Worst Excuse for an Actual Movie (All Concept/No Content). The film's U.S. commercial release failed to earn back its bloated $109 million budget, but overseas turnout enabled the film to squeak out the slightest of profits.

However, that was not enough to charm the Dr. Seuss estate; plans for a sequel were cancelled and, to date, no further live-action adaptations of the Dr. Seuss canon have been allowed by the author's executors.

Catwoman
(2004, directed by Pitof)

ARGUABLY THE MOST BELOVED female villain of the comic book genre is Catwoman, the sexy miscreant who bedeviled Batman. The 1960s *Batman* television series and movie spin-off brought the character to life via high-camp performances by the likes of Julie Newmar, Lee Meriwether, and Eartha Kitt. In the 1990s cinematic reboot of the Batman franchise, Michelle Pfeiffer took on the role and carried on the tradition of the so-bad-she's-*purr*fect Catwoman.

For this 2004 film version, the character's original backstory as a cat burglar named Selina Kyle was tossed aside in favor of a new plot that reinvented the lady as a crime fighter with superhero powers. Actually, this extreme revisionism was the least of the film's many problems.

Catwoman focuses on Patience Phillips, a graphic designer for a cosmetics company. She discovers that one of the company's products has toxic side effects and the corporate leadership opts to kill her before she reveals this dangerous secret to the authorities. Patience is left for dead, but is revived by a mysterious Egyptian Mau cat sent by the goddess Bast. Patience develops superpowers of a feline variety (including the ability to leap across great lengths and survive falls from significant heights) and she dons a dominatrix-style costume to become Catwoman. Her first crime-fighting assignment, not surprisingly, involves vengeance against her former employers.

Several high-profile actresses, including Ashley Judd and Nicole Kidman, flirted with the role before rejecting it. Halle Berry, fresh off her Academy Award victory for *Monster's Ball*, was recruited for the part.

Unfortunately, *Catwoman* emerged as a film that was seriously at odds with itself. The screenplay seemed corny and trite and French-born director Pitof's attempts to pump life into the enervated story via music video-style direction only called further attention to the poverty of the core material.

Berry, normally a charismatic performer who was no stranger to action flicks, seemed strangely ill at ease with the role's requirements. As a result of her weak performance, the film was dominated by the full-throttle overacting of Sharon Stone and Lambert Wilson as the cosmetic company executives who tried to have Patience killed. A violent climax between Berry and Stone created a surplus of unintentional chuckles instead of action/adventure thrills with neither actress making a good impression as fighters.

The critics, not surprisingly, went overboard with feline-style puns to slam the film with the Catholic News Service's Henry Herx going the furthest by referring to the flick as "kitty litter." Warner Bros. was not laughing when the $100 million production failed to come anywhere close to a profit, but Berry managed to earn the last laugh after her performance snagged an unflattering (albeit deserved) Razzie Award. She made a surprise appearance at the Razzies ceremony with her *Monster's Ball* Oscar and graciously accepted her Razzie with a speech that cheerfully acknowledged her bomb.

"First of all, I want to thank Warner Brothers," Berry said, barely controlling her own laughter. "Thank you for putting me in a piece of shit, god-awful movie… It was just what my career needed!"

Chariots of the Gods
(1970, directed by Harald Reinl)

CHARIOTS OF THE GODS (originally titled *Memories of the Future*) occupies an uneasy position that can easily embarrass anyone interested in the use of cinema as a vehicle for nonfiction filmmaking. A 1970 German production that, incredibly, received an Academy Award nomination for Best Documentary, the film turned up in U.S. theaters in 1974 via the tiny Sun International distribution company. Unlike most documentary distributors of the period, Sun International heavily promoted this title via a noisy television advertising campaign and a tie-in with a paperback reissue of the hitherto obscure Erich von Däniken text that served as its source material.

The aggressive marketing campaign, coupled with the decision to put the film into wide general release rather than limited art house distribution, helped make the film a commercial hit. It also managed to kick off a craze for film and television productions that insisted on hitherto unexplored connections between human cultures and unidentified extraterrestrials that allegedly made mysterious visits to our planet.

As for the film itself, *Chariots of the Gods* is a droning slice of endless speculation that suggests the ancient cultures of Egypt, Central America, and Easter Island were incapable of creating any significant architectural, artistic, or mechanical invention without the aid of experts who came from beyond the stars. At the very least, it is a typical example of Eurocentric boorishness—obviously, the creators of Stonehenge or the glories of ancient Greece and Rome had the brains, tools, and muscles to move and sculpt huge chunks of stone into fancy upright designs whereas their cousins across the Mediterranean and the Atlantic did not.

At worst, the film provides a careless pondering that shuffles about without an iota of evidence that any spaceships ever landed on Earth. There is talk of supposedly ancient airports at Nazca in Peru, but no proof that any vehicle actually touched down. There is wonderment at the marvels of the Mayan and Incan ruins, but no explanation of how aliens could have passed on their engineering knowledge to a supposedly primitive people—consider the language barrier at the very least.

The film points to a number of different sacred religious texts, including the stories of Moses, Ezekiel, and Elijah in the Old Testament, with their vivid descriptions of chariots coming down from the heavens and then flying away. Yet almost every religious tradition is rooted in some sense of the supernatural descending from a higher plane, both literally and figuratively, to enlighten the supposed dullards of Earth.

Chariots of the Gods never overtly claims that aliens were running around the ancient world—after all, no physical remains of ancient extraterrestrials have ever been presented. Instead, it broadly hints that the combination of unusual religious stories and funky structures around most of the world may suggest that otherworldly visitors came by to share insights and ideas. However, there is no explanation as to why these visitors never bothered to return.

In terms of style, the film has little to offer. Director Harald Reinl is satisfied to stitch together stock footage of rocket ships in flight, atomic bombs in mushroom-shaped clouds of destructiveness, and endless aerial shots of celebrated ancient monuments.

Part found footage, part travelogue, fully ridiculous, yet strangely naïve in making claims it cannot possibly defend, *Chariots of the Gods* is a charming old-school fraud. They don't make films like this anymore and we should be glad for that.

Che!
(1969, directed by Richard Fleischer)

ERNESTO "CHE" GUEVARA died in 1967, yet continues to fascinate and puzzle a world in desperate search of heroes. With his shaggy hair, brooding gaze, and fascinating mix of intellectualism and armed rebellion, Guevara is the ultimate antihero. However, with this biopic, you come away knowing very little about the enigmatic revolutionary and learning too much about bad filmmaking.

The main problem with *Che!* was the film's obvious unease about embracing an individual who openly espoused Marxist revolution. Even in the hippy-dippy late 1960s, Hollywood was not about to wave the red flag with lusty abandon. To appease the still-conservative Middle America moviegoers while appealing to the left-of-center youth who made Guevara a martyr, *Che!* tried to do the impossible by extracting the eponymous subject's politics from nearly all of the film. As a result, Guevara comes across like a causeless rebel—he's fighting for vague ideas, not for a clearly defined political agenda.

Also, *Che!* is not a very thorough biopic. It opens during the Cuban Revolution when Guevara was part of Castro's ragtag army in their war to overthrow the Batista dictatorship. No hint of Guevara's Argentine past is brought up outside of a passing reference that he preferred his country's tea to Cuban coffee. The film also avoids Guevara's role in the Cuban government under Castro, ignores his failed attempt to create a Marxist revolution in the Congo, and barely considers the political roots of the revolutionary actions that led to his demise in the Bolivian jungles. Call it *Che!*-lite.

The result of that strategy makes the film completely confusing in regards to understanding what made Guevara tick politically. But, in a strange way, that is a blessing since it allows the viewer to enjoy some unexpected camp—after all, how often do you find Che Guevara and Fidel Castro being played for unintentional laughs?

For no clear reason, it was decided to cast Omar Sharif (complete with an Egyptian accent) as Guevara and Jack Palance (under *very* heavy makeup) as Castro.

As with Guevara, the film's Castro never talks Red politics until late in the movie and even then, he comes across more as a stooge to the Soviets than a serious Communist ideologue. Thus, you can watch *Che!* and have no clue as to why Castro and Guevara went to war to overthrow the Batista dictatorship and why they terrified John F. Kennedy and every administration that followed.

So what do you have in *Che!* instead? Well, you have a bunch of motley extras in nondescript soldier uniforms running about in a jungle setting, occasionally shooting guns into the distance. You have repeated scenes of extras being tied up, blindfolded, and shot in firing squads. You have white actors in thick greasepaint who are supposed to be Cubans. You have people looking straight into the camera and talking about the Che they knew and either loved or hated. You have snippets of newsreel footage laced with clumsy re-creations of actual events (including Palance's Castro giving dramatic speeches to cheering masses). And you have some rather well-known Puerto Rican landmarks doubling as Cuban landmarks.

Ultimately, in *Che!* you have… a mess.

Christabel
(2002, directed by James Fotopoulos)

FOR THOSE WHO ACTIVELY LOATHE experimental cinema, please avoid James Fotopoulos's *Christabel* at all costs. And for those who actively love experimental cinema… well, the same advice applies.

Yeah, that is a bit of an extreme opening paragraph. But this obscurity is so utterly and thoroughly bizarre that it is impossible to view it without wondering what the hell is going on.

Christabel is billed as a "loose adaptation of the poem by Samuel Taylor Coleridge." If this adaptation were any looser, it would fall off the screen. Coleridge's haunting yet unfinished text is presented here as a muck of overlapping images of two young women, distorted sounds, some kind of noise which may or may not be music, and occasional slices of Coleridge's poem read in a muffled, barely audible voice.

Every now and then, a nude woman walks across the screen and the camera focuses on her breasts—perhaps in tribute to the pleasure domes of another Coleridge poem?

The *Christabel* press kit promised a "film drenched in sexual imagery" and insists that "Fotopoulos boldly focuses on iconic images of the women themselves rather than on their actions or the narrative as it unfolds between them." While viewers will not need to towel themselves off from being "drenched in sexual imagery" (the silly women of *Christabel* spend a surplus amount of their time wandering around and making faces at the camera instead of luxuriating in erotic splendor), the press kit deserves kudos for being honest in admitting the film has no action or narrative.

James Fotopoulos is a wildly prolific filmmaker who created four features and twenty-one shorts in the nine years before *Christabel* was made and he has since gone on to create critically acclaimed works of avant-garde art. Hey, everyone is entitled to at least one anti-classic!

The Conqueror
(1956, directed by Dick Powell)

Few movies have carried the simultaneous burdens of campy stupidity and crass tragedy more than this wildly misguided RKO disaster on the rise of the Mongol warrior-leader Genghis Khan.

Way back in thirteenth-century Asia, the Mongol chief Temujin kidnaps the daughter of a Tartar princess, which leads to a bloody war that culminates in Temujin's rise to power as Genghis Khan. For reasons that no one could fathom at the time, John Wayne believed he was born to play Temujin and with Charlie Chan–style makeup, he barely turned himself into the physical representation of a Mongol warrior (he kept his trademark western drawl for his line readings). And if Wayne was no one's idea of a Mongol, red-haired and fair-skinned Susan Hayward created an equally peculiar concept of what a Tartar princess supposedly resembled.

Actor Dick Powell took on the directing chores even though he was ill equipped to bring a sprawling historic epic to the screen. The resulting film provides a weird mix of a violent romantic relation between the leads along with various subplots of court intrigue and military bravado by a Caucasian cast that wore yellow face makeup and tacky pseudo-Asian costumes.

Since filming in then-Communist Mongolia was out of the question, Powell and producer Howard Hughes chose the desert near St. George, Utah, to stand in for the Asian landscapes. After location shooting was completed, sixty tons of Utah soil were shipped back to RKO in order to provide a visual continuity for the studio-based sequences.

Alas, the inanity of the miscast movie was destroyed by an extraordinary tragedy: the St. George location was downwind from the U.S. government's Nevada National Security Site, where above-ground nuclear testing took place three years before the cast and crew of *The Conqueror* arrived to make their film. The radioactive soil wreaked havoc on the production's principals: Powell, Wayne, and Hayward all died of cancer, as well as supporting actors Agnes Moorehead and John Hoyt. Mexican actor Pedro Armendáriz committed suicide in 1963 after receiving a cancer diagnosis. All told, ninety-one members of the cast and crew developed some form of cancer by 1981 with forty-six dying from the disease.

After Hughes sold RKO, he bought back the rights to *The Conqueror* and secured every available print of the film. Whether this was based on his guilt over the film's high rate of cancer deaths or whether it was because he liked the film is unclear (he also bought up the rights and prints to another of his anti-classic films, the John Wayne aerial adventure *Jet Pilot*). After Hughes's death, *The Conqueror* was rereleased and it confirmed everyone's fears. Yes, it was a marvelously ridiculous production. But the death count attached to its mayhem made it difficult to fully appreciate the depth of its buffoonery.

The Creeping Terror
(1964, directed by Vic Savage, credited as A. J. Nelson)

DURING THE 1950S AND 1960S, America's grind houses and drive-ins were overrun with low-budget screamfests where marauding monsters, antagonistic aliens, and various creatures waged war on Earth's seemingly puny human population. After a while, all of these films seemed to look and sound alike. However, *The Creeping Terror* stands apart for its overwhelming sense of inertia—rarely has a sci-fi/horror flick been so disturbing for its total sense of pure enervation.

On the surface, the film is strictly standard issue: An alien spaceship lands in a small, isolated town and a creature emerges with an insatiable appetite for humans. In this case, though, the creature is a long, hairy, and strangely slow-moving entity—the Medved Brothers, in their 1986 book *Son of the Golden Turkey Awards*, facetiously claim the creature is a giant carpet from outer space.

The creature also consumes an abnormally high number of people. This has been explained by the film's bizarre backstory. The film is the creation of Arthur N. White, a Connecticut-born con man who used the name "A. J. Nelson" for his directing and producing credits and "Vic Savage" for his starring role as the heroic sheriff. White/Nelson/Savage managed to secure funds from private investors, who agreed to help finance the film if they played the roles of the alien's victims. Hence, the hairy thing from another galaxy had to eat up everyone who put money into *The Creeping Terror*. White/Nelson/Savage departed with the film's finances before the film was completed. One of the film's stars, actor/model William Thourlby, managed to locate the footage before it was lost and piece it together.

Unfortunately for the viewer, *The Creeping Terror* was shot without sound—White/Nelson/Savage claimed that he would dub the dialogue in later. As a result, the entire film carries an off-screen narration that details every thought, emotion, and action that occurs on-screen. Truly, you've never experienced anything so bizarre as watching a feature-length film where a single male voice provides all of the dialogue and an endless commentary concerning the on-screen action, especially when the narrator goes into excessive overdrive to explain the tension between two of the male leads.

"Barney and Martin had been bachelor buddies for years," says the narrator. "But now that Martin was settling down to marriage, they were slowly drifting apart. Barney, naturally, was still dating all the girls in town and he couldn't understand why Brett and Martin didn't pal around with him more than they did. He couldn't comprehend that married life brought with it not only new problems and duties, but the necessary togetherness of husband and wife as well. Despite Brett's most tactful considerations, such as inviting him over to dinner quite often, Barney was growing resentful of her or at least she felt that he was. Since time began, this change in relationships probably happened to all buddies in similar circumstances. Life has its way of making boys grow up and, with marriage, Martin's time had come. His life was now Brett, a life that he thoroughly enjoyed."

The film also has a grisly trivia footnote: assistant director Randy Starr would become notorious five years later as the person who provided the Manson family with the gun used in the Tate-LaBianca murders.

The elusive White/Nelson/Savage reportedly died in Kansas City of liver failure in 1975 or so the Internet Movie Database claims; as of this writing, no independent confirmation of his fate has surfaced. His life and *The Creeping Terror* became the subject of the appropriately titled 2011 documentary *Creep!*

Dance Hall Racket
(1953, directed by Phil Tucker)

DURING THE PEAK YEARS of his career, Lenny Bruce was such a controversial figure that no Hollywood studio dared to consider him for on-screen film work. But that's not to say Bruce didn't dream of movie stardom. Alas, his sole effort to gain a foothold as a movie star has been widely maligned as being one of the worst films of the 1950s: *Dance Hall Racket*, which Bruce also wrote.

On the surface, *Dance Hall Racket* is a simple story: a sleazy dance hall is used as the cover for a gem-smuggling operation. An undercover government agent infiltrates the setting, but infighting among the various parties within the operation helps to speed up its downfall.

But *Dance Hall Racket* goes far beyond that benign setting into a deeper tapestry of offbeat personalities who populate the dance hall. Umberto Scalli, the suave owner of the establishment, runs a tight ship and doesn't think twice about dispatching his goons, Icepick and Vinnie, to maintain order. Within the dance hall, a variety of young girls express rue and indifference to their less-than-glamorous jobs of entertaining a variety of bums, dreamers, and losers. An older dance hall employee serves as a mother hen to the girls, giving them encouragement to make the best of their dubious employment.

Around the dance hall's bar are a variety of inebriates and sad souls drowning their disappointments in booze and broads. One man is determined to save up enough dance tickets so he can have full run of the establishment for one night where he would be able to keep other patrons out and have the girls to himself. Another man, a drunken Swede, goes to elaborate lengths to steal drinks from unsuspecting patrons and the agitated bartender.

Bruce is often considered the star of the film, but in truth, *Dance Hall Racket* has no single star to fuel it. In fact, Bruce (playing the goon Vinnie) has a small role; Timothy Farrell, as Umberto Scalli, has more screen time.

Watching *Dance Hall Racket* today, it is a major shame that Bruce's intensive screenplay wasn't provided to a better production outfit. Exploitation producer George Weiss kept the film in an ultra-low budget setting (it looks as if it was shot in someone's basement) while hack director Phil Tucker, best known for the egregious *Robot Monster*, had no clue how to frame a shot.

Of course, there's Lenny Bruce. Admittedly, he is miscast as the too-tough Vinnie—can you imagine Lenny Bruce as a switchblade-swinging, karate-chopping nut job who is pathologically jealous of his girlfriend? Even if he was the wrong man for the part, it is impossible not to admire Bruce's willingness to step outside of his well-defined comic persona and attempt to inhabit an unusual dramatic role.

Bruce's mother, Sally Marr, and his wife, Honey Harlow, were also part of the cast, which gives the film a warped home movie vibe.

A Dirty Shame
(2004, directed by John Waters)

JOHN WATERS'S NC-17-RATED FILM *A Dirty Shame* is easily the most surprising comedy of his career. The surprise: it's not funny. And for a John Waters film, that is highly unusual.

The film certainly had the potential for being hilarious. Set in a less fashionable section of Baltimore, the story finds the local population split into two segments. There are the sexual libertines who don't hesitate to explore their lust and flaunt their fetishes in public and there are the self-described neuters that hold decency rallies in an attempt to restore rigid Puritanism to society. In the middle of this is Sylvia Stickles (Tracey Ullman), a grouchy convenience store owner who has no patience or desire for sex. When she receives a concussion in a freak car accident, she becomes driven into extreme new directions by suddenly overcharged carnal desires.

Sylvia's husband (Chris Isaak) is initially happy with his wife's thawing out from frigidity, but then he becomes seriously bothered by her embrace of free love. Sylvia is pegged as a new apostle for a band of sex addicts led by the auto mechanic Ray Ray Perkins (Johnny Knoxville), who has Christ-like talents for curing the sick and raising the dead (including a squirrel who is revived by mouth-to-mouth resuscitation), but this healer goes the extra mile by refueling their sex engines to roar off into new horizons.

The real shame in *A Dirty Shame* is a wonderful setup and a dismal execution. Waters basically conceived a dozen smutty jokes and spends eighty-eight minutes repeating them endlessly. Typical is Sylvia's daughter Caprice (Selma Blair), who has mammoth mammary glands and performs go-go dancing in a biker bar as Ursula Udders. The sight gag of Selma Blair sporting Chesty Morgan–worthy tits is amusing… for thirty seconds. But after a while, watching her shake the (obviously) fake breasts is not funny. It is repetitious and boring—and when big breasts are boring, you know something is wrong.

Likewise, the film is populated with fetishistic characters that exist solely for endless displays of outrageousness. Watching a fat cop indulge in adult infantilism (complete with pacifier and baby clothing) is okay as a one-shot gag. But by the thirtieth goo-goo-ga-ga, it is painful. Or having a trio of husky, hairy men identify themselves as bears can be mildly silly when they first make their presence known (they initially greet their neighbors as being Mama, Papa, and Baby Bear), but after the fifteenth growling bear reference, you'd wish these ursine men would hibernate and let some genuinely inventive characters show up on-screen.

The film does have one (and only one) inspired moment when Ullman's character, suddenly liberated with a new degree of sexual audacity, visits a nursing home and joins the seniors in a line dance of the "Hokey Pokey." She takes the song's lyrics too literally when she begins to shake it all about, transforming a simple kiddie dance tune into a brazen display of unleashed eroticism which culminates in Ullman lifting a water bottle from the floor with her vagina. This is genuine old-style John Waters: grotesque in concept, yet gorgeous in the happy disregard for taste and manners. But, sadly, the moment is too brief to make a dent on the monotony.

Dogarama
(1971, directed by Lawrence T. Cole)

IN 1972, the X-rated feature *Deep Throat* became the surprise sensation of the year. A great deal of the media fascination with this unlikely production centered on its charming leading lady, the hitherto unknown Linda Lovelace. Indeed, Lovelace's fame became so pronounced that she was welcomed as a guest on Johnny Carson's *Tonight Show* and as a prominent audience member at the next year's Academy Awards ceremony.

But as Lovelace's celebrity grew, strange whispers began percolating about another movie starring the clothing-free lady. Unlike the loopy softcore comedy of *Deep Throat*, the other film ventured into the unpleasant taboo territory of bestiality. Lovelace initially claimed to be unaware of any such film, but she eventually acknowledged its existence after prints began to surface.

The film in question was shot in 1971 and has been released under a variety of titles, including one that is inappropriate for publication in a family-friendly surrounding, but it is perhaps best known as *Dogarama*. This production is something of a legend in pornography history and while many people have heard about the film, relatively few have actually seen it.

Dogarama was one of a seemingly endless number of "loops" produced in the early 1970s. Loops were short 8mm porno flicks that were made quickly and cheaply for distribution in the growing number of X-rated theaters and peep show venues that proliferated in American cities; some loops were also sold through mail-order catalogs in violation of the U.S. postal laws of the era. The loops had little in the way of artistic value and there was a certain sense of seen-one-seen-them-all to their offerings.

With *Dogarama*, however, things were a little different. Rather than concentrate on male-female sex, this loop introduced a canine participant into the carnal romp. It is unclear who came up with this idea, but even in the raucous early 1970s, this concept was more than a little extreme.

Dogarama begins with a fairly typical porno scenario with Lovelace and reigning X-rated stud Eric Edwards enjoying each other's company. Or, at least here, he is having more fun than she is. When Edwards is satisfied, he abruptly dresses and departs, leaving poor Lovelace in a most unsatisfactory mood.

Ah, but sexual salvation awaits her via the trusty pet dog. This happy bow-bow—it is not certain whether it is a German shepherd or an Alsatian—appears to take his job as man's best friend very, very seriously. For the remainder of the film, the viewer is treated to glimpses of Lovelace showing more than a maternal interest in the dog while the four-legged star reciprocates with several aggressive displays of (what else?) doggie-style sex.

Dogarama will come as a shock for anyone who is unfamiliar with this extreme form of deviant pornography. The film provides extreme close-ups of Lovelace pleasuring the pooch in a variety of ways and the poor animal plays alpha dog to his willing human partner. Anyone with a weak stomach should stay as far from *Dogarama* as possible.

But at the same time, this is also a weirdly confusing endeavor and in its excessive awfulness, it raises a host of questions that will puzzle the sensitive viewer. For instance, did anyone making this film genuinely believe that people would find this stuff erotic or even amusing? Was some sort of sick statement being made with *Dogarama* that equated women with pet dogs? Did the notion of animal abuse come into play during the planning stages of the film? And, quite frankly, how did people react when they ambled into X-rated venues in 1971 and witnessed this unlikely spectacle?

The story behind the film—and, for that matter, Lovelace's relatively brief porno career—has been the subject of considerable debate. Lovelace, as stated earlier, initially denied ever being in the film. When *Screw* magazine publisher Al Goldstein obtained a print and published screen freezes, she accused him of faking the stills in order to cash in on her fame. But the curiosity about the flick never evaporated and Lovelace would be unhappily reacquainted with the film during a visit to the Playboy Mansion when Hugh Hefner admitted that he had a print in his private film collection.

Lovelace would eventually be forced to say that she participated in the film and in a second (but lesser-known) loop that included another go-round of sex with a dog. However, in her 1980 autobiography, *Ordeal*, she would insist that she was violently coerced by her then-husband, Chuck Traynor, to make love to a dog on camera. Lovelace accused Traynor of inflicting a "brutal beating" and threatening her with a gun prior to the shoot and she sought to expunge the memory of the film by claiming its creation was the most painful moment of her life.

Ironically, *Dogarama* would never have been recalled had *Deep Throat* not become a cultural phenomenon and Linda Lovelace not become a household name. To borrow a line from Brad Pitt: Fame is a bitch, man!

Don's Plum
(2001, directed by R. D. Robb)

In December 2004, Leonardo DiCaprio and Tobey Maguire received an unwanted Christmas gift: a sixteen-page lawsuit from the co-producer of a 1996 no-budget movie called *Don's Plum*, which featured the two megastars as part of an ensemble cast. The lawsuit, filed by one John Schindler, said DiCaprio and Maguire "have intentionally interfered with the exhibition and distribution" of the movie by stating their opposition to the commercial release of the film, thus scaring away potential distributors.

This was not the first time that *Don's Plum* was dragged into court. An earlier suit by another producer of the film, David Stutman, against the two stars was settled in September 1999. Stutman made the same claim as Schindler, but was able to wrest a compromise that allowed *Don's Plum* to be released everywhere except the United States and Canada.

So what is the big deal over this little movie? *Don's Plum* took six days to shoot (three in 1995 and three the following year). Quite frankly, it looks it. Shot in a grimy black-and-white 16mm, the action centers on a Los Angeles diner where a group of slackers in their early twenties gather for an evening of stale food and scatological conversation.

The link to the circle are the guys: Derek (Leonardo DiCaprio), a chain-smoking wise-ass who doesn't think twice about openly insulting people within earshot at other tables; Brad (Scott Bloom), a sensitive guy with crystal-blue eyes; Ian (Tobey Maguire), a vegetarian goofball whose high-pitched voice and clownish demeanor recall the character of Screech on the TV show *Saved by the Bell*; and Jeremy (Kevin Connolly), an aspiring actor. Joining the guys is Brad's current girlfriend, Sara (Jenny Lewis), who is shocked to hear of Brad's gay tendencies, but who herself later turns Sapphic when her pal Constance (Heather McComb) turns up and joins the table. Ian invites a waitress, Juliet (Meadow Sisto), from a jazz club while Jeremy arrives with a hitchhiking hippie named Amy (Amber Benson).

And then, once everyone is seated, *Don's Plum* dribbles endlessly in no clear direction. Much of the film was reportedly improvised, which may explain why so much time is devoted to foul language, name calling, and in-depth descriptions of masturbation, oral sex, homosexual encounters, sex-for-hire, drug use, and family scandals. Within the course of a ninety-minute roundtable over coffee, cola, and French fries, the characters begin to unveil various secrets which respectively plagued them: a father's suicide, molestation by a sleazy uncle, narcotic addiction, a hitherto unannounced gay lifestyle, etc. At various points, the characters retreat one at a time to a bathroom and speak to themselves in the mirror about the action going on around them.

Don's Plum looks and plays like a student film made by ambitious young people who never experienced life. It would have been lost in obscurity except for a little movie called *Titanic*. With DiCaprio as the self-proclaimed king of the world, followed later by Maguire's star ascension in *The Ice Storm* and *The Cider House Rules,* the producers of the half-forgotten *Don's Plum* dusted off their movie with the hopes of bringing it to theaters.

However, DiCaprio and Maguire worked to keep the movie off the screen, claiming that their appearances in *Don's Plum* were strictly intended as a "favor to a friend" under "the express agreement that it would never be exhibited as a feature-length motion picture." (These quotes come from the original legal maneuvers.)

Not unlike many legal tug-of-wars, this case is the proverbial much ado about nothing. Frankly, this plum isn't especially juicy and without DiCaprio and Maguire, no one would want to pluck it. Still, this should be a lesson to any aspiring movie superstar: Be careful of the little projects that you make along the path to glory because they might return to haunt you and enrich your attorneys!

Don't Worry, We'll Think of a Title
(1966, directed by Harmon Jones)

THE YEAR 1966 was a crucial one for funnyman Morey Amsterdam. Up until that point, his performance on the long-running sitcom *The Dick Van Dyke Show* and his appearances in the popular *Beach Party* movies brought him to wide and appreciative audiences. Yet Amsterdam was pretty much a second banana in those projects, which must have been an ego blow to someone who had previously been a headliner in clubs and on TV (he was a forgotten pioneer in late-night programming with the show *Broadway Open House* in the late 1940s).

Recruiting his fellow *Dick Van Dyke Show* second banana castmates Rose Marie and Richard Deacon, Amsterdam decided to produce, write, and star in a motion picture. He embarked on a project that most people have charitably viewed as a debacle: *Don't Worry, We'll Think of a Title*.

Amsterdam and Rose Marie play a cook and waitress in a crappy diner run by Deacon, who is on the receiving end of their inept shenanigans from the get-go. In the first twenty minutes of the film, he gets whipped cream squirted in his face, a pancake planted on his bald cranium, and a cake placed on his chair.

Fired for gross incompetence, Amsterdam and Rose Marie are hired by an ex-colleague who inherited a bookstore in a college town. But as luck would have it, Amsterdam is mistaken by Communist agents for Yasha Nudnik, a defecting cosmonaut, and a group of Red spies try to abduct him to find out the whereabouts of various state secrets.

Director Harmon Jones specialized in B-level exploitation (most notably *Gorilla at Large* and *The Beast of Budapest*), but he had no clue how to frame a comedy. Since there was no budget for elaborate comedy gags or chases, Amsterdam dipped into his Borscht Belt joke book and came up with an endless skein of horrible jokes and one-liners. Here is some of the dialogue that he dropped in the movie:

> RESTAURANT PATRON: Do you think I could have duck eggs?
> MOREY AMSTERDAM: You could if you were a duck.
>
> RESTAURANT PATRON: (trying to attract Rose Marie): Girlie! Girlie!
> ROSE MARIE: Did you call me, sir?
> RESTAURANT PATRON: No, I called you Girlie.
>
> MOREY AMSTERDAM: Did I tell you I had a cousin who was a bookkeeper? Every time he borrows a book, he keeps it.

And those are the funnier jokes! If the film ran longer, Amsterdam would've been forced to include knock-knock jokes to pad the footage.

Realizing the material was more than a little dubious, Amsterdam corralled a number of prominent TV stars to make gag appearances. Thus the film is polluted by the likes of Danny Thomas (nearly being knocked over by a chicken), Milton Berle (dragging a rope through the bookstore), Steve Allen (looking for a book called *The Sex Life of Armadilloes*), Forrest Tucker (seducing a woman in the diner), Cliff Arquette (as his beloved Charlie Weaver character), Irene Ryan (as Granny from *The Beverly Hillbillies*), and ex-*Dick Van Dyke Show* alum Carl Reiner (extolling the virtues of his toupee). One of the spies in the film gets in touch via walkie-talkie with "James Bond," although the voice responding over airwaves sounds more like Nigel Bruce's Doctor Watson rather than Sean Connery's machismo Scottish growl. There's even a snippet of cartoon featuring Sylvester the Cat tossed in.

But the strangest cameo belongs to Moe Howard, who shows up without the other Stooges in a totally straight role as a lawyer. Why? Who knows?

The Dragon Lives Again
(1977, directed by Law Kei)

IT IS IMPOSSIBLE TO THINK of a more unlikely tribute to the martial arts superstar Bruce Lee than the 1977 fantasy *The Dragon Lives Again*. This is the rare kung fu caper that would probably be more at home in a surrealist film festival rather than a martial arts roundup.

The Dragon Lives Again follows Bruce Lee into his life after death. The mysterious circumstances of his death are not discussed, but never mind. Poor Bruce Lee winds up in The Underworld, which is a predominantly Chinese purgatory approximately one flight up from Hell. The Underworld is run by a king who wears a beaded lampshade on his head and chases naked concubines around a giant hot tub (nice work if you can get it).

It seems that the king is facing a possible coup by a variety of '60s and '70s pop culture icons that want to take over The Underworld. This gang includes James Bond (a bushy-haired white guy in a cheap tuxedo), Clint Eastwood (a Chinese guy with a beard, wearing the poncho costume from the Leone westerns), the Exorcist (another Chinese guy, wearing a black Nehru jacket), Zaitoichi the Blind Swordsman (who simulates his ocular disability by fluttering his eyelids), and Emmanuelle (the happy hedonist of French soft-core porn). There is also a Chinese Dracula who seems to have overcome his Transylvanian counterpart's aversion to sunlight.

Bruce Lee, however, recruits his own gang of good guys to fight this evil band. Part of the heroic team is the fabled One-Armed Boxer (whom Bruce casually refers to as "One-Armed") and Popeye the Sailor. Yes, Popeye the Sailor is here... at least in the form of a Chinese guy with a shaved head, a large corncob pipe, and the Popeye costume. This Popeye doesn't need spinach, however, as he handles villains by squeezing their noses and pushing them by their faces into walls.

Adding to the chaos is the presence of Bruce Leong as Bruce Lee. Leong (real name: Hsiao Liang) bears no physical resemblance whatsoever to the man he is supposed to portray. The filmmakers were obviously aware of this drawback, thus prefacing his entrance into the action by having the supporting female characters comment that the lack of resemblance is expected since people are physically transformed after death and so have different appearances.

Leong also doesn't conduct his martial arts moves in a manner that recalls the original Lee. Indeed, the movie's silly fight sequences consist of a surplus of air punches and slaps that miss their bodily target by a good measure while the soundtrack chokes up with Three Stooges–style sound effects of pokes, bangs, and knocks.

Even more curious is the fact that *The Dragon Lives Again* takes more than a few minutes to talk about a celebrated aspect of Bruce Lee that never found its way into camera range during his lifetime. There is a lot of conversation among the concubines about the high number of women eager to have hoochy-koo with Bruce Lee and one of the admiring ladies comments on the late star's manhood with the immortal line: "When a man's endowed like Bruce, the girls are bound to want him." Sadly, the film never puts its money shot where its mouth is and Bruce's only fling with the ladies comes when the wicked Emmanuelle tries seduction tactics by dancing the mazurka with him in her bedroom.

For its American release, *The Dragon Lives Again* was dubbed into English by people who probably never saw the film they were asked to loop. The Exorcist is inexplicably given a French accent, the king's advisers sound like Alvin and the Chipmunks, and Bruce Lee is given a Noo Yawk honk that makes him sound like Leo Gorcey. Popeye is not given a voice equal to the cartoon original, but instead has a slightly Chinese-accented speaking voice.

What any of this has to do with Bruce Lee's legacy is never entirely clear, but when you have a scenario where Clint Eastwood and James Bond are trying to take over a Chinese purgatory and Bruce Lee calls on Popeye the Sailor to help save the day (not counting the interlude where the cast talks about Bruce Lee's penis), it would seem that cogent and coherent thought was not high on the filmmakers' priority list.

The Driver's Seat
(1974, directed by Giuseppe Patroni Griffi)

THIS FILM, which is based on a novella by the celebrated British writer Muriel Spark, is supposed to be a psychological thriller about an introverted woman's rapid descent into delusion and self-destructiveness. However, Elizabeth Taylor, who was not exactly an introverted personality, plays the character with such an uncontrolled, crazy performance that was considered ballistic even by her hammy late-career standards. It is not surprising that the All-Movie Guide dubbed this her worst movie.

The problems actually begin with the opening credits, which identify the film as *The Driver's Seat (Identikit)*. Why the film needs two titles is unclear.

The film opens with a surreal and creepy visit to a dress shop filled with mannequins that don't have clothing, but have silver foil wrapped around their heads. Taylor's character Lise is there to buy a dress, but she inexplicably goes berserk when the salesgirl informs her that the desired dress is stain resistant. She is only mollified when she is given a dress that is not stain resistant.

From there, Lise prepares to go on a trip to Rome, but her encounters with sex-obsessed travelers create a disruptive and stressful trip. Lise escapes to the airport security check-in station. Annoyed by the inspections, she holds her handbag aloft and declares: "This may look like a purse, but it is actually a bomb!" At this point in the film, Taylor's voice seems to go several decibels higher than normal and all of her lines from here out are screamed.

Getting into the airplane, Lise fastens her safety belt and moans with slight orgiastic glee at being locked in for takeoff. A weird man sits next to her with a big, lascivious grin on his face. She sneers and yells: "You look like Red Riding Hood's grandmother. Do you want to eat me?" The man grins wider and replies: "I'd like to, I'd like to. But I'm on a macrobiotic diet and I can't eat meat."

Once in Rome, Lise runs into Andy Warhol, shares a taxi with a Jehovah's Witness, watches the bombing assassination of an Arab diplomat, is sexually assaulted by a hunky mechanic, and then makes the acquaintance of a local creep who can satisfy her ultimate self-destructive wish.

Director Giuseppe Patroni Griffi doesn't seem to be in control of the movie. He is certainly not directing Taylor: She is running amok with wild gazes, a shrieking voice, spastic body language, and the refusal to stop acting like a movie queen. Whether complaining over a dirty glass, ogling cute men, sifting through a collection of scarves in a department store display, or surrendering herself to sexual abandon, she engages in the most extravagant hamming ever put on camera. It is not acting, to be certain, but it is highly amusing and is so blatantly wrong that it never ceases to entertain.

If that's not odd enough, the film is burdened with bizarre artistic touches. Griffi makes a Roman police interrogation room look like the set for a music video, complete with harsh white lights and expressionistic interior decorating. There is also a piano score that is supposed to set the off-kilter mood for the thriller, but which instead sounds like a kitten romping across the ivories. As the film is populated with an Italian cast, the English version is dubbed with voices that never fit their Roman mouths.

The Driver's Seat is a true so-bad-it's-fun experience. Anyone who needs a healthy dose of wild turkey cinema will do well to jump on this funhouse ride.

Empire
(1964, directed by Andy Warhol)

ON JULY 25, 1964, the New York office of Henry Romney, vice president of the Rockefeller Foundation, was abuzz with activity. Andy Warhol, the reigning king of the pop art movement, and filmmaker Jonas Mekas arrived to shoot a movie; Gerard Malanga, Marie Desert, and John Palmer accompanied them that night. The office's location—the forty-first floor of the Time-Life Building—was of prime importance because it offered an unobstructed view of the Empire State Building.

Warhol and Mekas pointed an Auricon 16mm sound camera through an office window at the Empire State Building. Beginning at 8:06 P.M. and lasting until 2:42 A.M., the duo filmed the celebrated skyscraper. Their Auricon camera held 1,200 feet of film in a single magazine, which required fourteen reel changes during the shoot.

The resulting film, *Empire*, became one of the most curious and controversial productions in the history of underground cinema. Although the film was shot with a sound camera at the normal 24fps speed, Warhol decided against using any soundtrack and insisted that *Empire* be shown at the silent-film projection speed of 16fps. As a result, *Empire* wound up with a ghastly running time of eight hours and five minutes. While that length might be suitable for a sprawling epic, it didn't seem to fit a production consisting of an unbroken gaze at an office building.

Empire opens with a white screen that quickly absorbs the image of the Empire State Building. During the film's first reel, the sun's light vanishes and the building's floodlights are turned on. For the rest of the film, the Empire State Building remains at the center of the screen—and that's pretty much all that happens. The only movement in the film comes from the occasional blinking of a tower light atop the Metropolitan Life Insurance Company building, which is seen behind the Empire State Building. In the film's final reel, the Empire State Building's floodlights go off and the only illumination comes from the lights atop the skyscraper's television broadcasting antenna.

For many years, *Empire* was famous by reputation only. Warhol presented a single exhibition of the film after its completion, but no theater or gallery would commit to playing it. Warhol refused to edit the film down and ordered that it never be shown in a truncated format. (In the past few years, New York's Museum of Modern Art, with the permission of the Warhol estate, occasionally showed a two-hour excerpt of the film.)

In the 1960s, many people dismissed *Empire* as a boring stunt. But time was ultimately Warhol's ally. In 2004, the Library of Congress caught many people off-guard by including *Empire* in the National Film Registry. Since then, a number of venues have dared to present the film in a single, intermission-free engagement. A few of these engagements have taken place in a traditional auditorium, most notably a highly publicized (though barely attended) 2011 screening at New York's Anthology Film Archives. The film has also been projected on the exterior walls of the Royal National Theatre in London in 2005 and Chicago's Aon Center in 2011.

During the past decade, *Empire* has generated speculation from film critics seeking to make sense of the work.

"Viewers quickly exhaust the visual information in the *Empire* frame; after a few minutes, they have nothing left to 'read' or interpret," writes film historian Daniel Eagan. "They can concentrate on the changes in the frame—building lights blink on and off, the flash frames caught on reel changes, the streaks made during film processing—but inevitably will find their minds wandering, unable to concentrate fully on an image that doesn't merit full attention. The building may start to lose in iconic power, to become a backdrop, a scenic element, something seen but not noticed outside a window."

"If, as has been argued, Warhol's Campbell's Soup can paintings and Brillo box sculptures transformed art-making from a physical into a philosophical act, then *Empire* could be said to do the same for filmmaking," writes Tom Vick of AllMovie.com. "With their long, fixed-perspective shots of mundane activities, Warhol's early '60s films constantly remind viewers that the camera is a machine capable of paying attention to anything for any length of time. *Empire* takes this idea to its absurd but logical extreme by asking its audience to commit this nearly impossible act of attention themselves. Warhol's abandonment of silent filmmaking soon after it was completed suggests that he too believed that *Empire* completed this stage of his filmmaking career."

My own view is not as eloquent or intensive. To be frank, I've never seen the entire *Empire*. But the eight-minute segment I saw in an unauthorized YouTube posting seemed like the full eight-hour endeavor. It was impossible to watch without yawning or getting agitated and, at the same time, it was also impossible to ignore.

For its sheer strangeness as a near-motionless motion picture, *Empire* is exasperating and amusing. And I suspect that is what Warhol was trying to achieve. When he was asked why he made such a bizarre work, Warhol claimed, "To see time go by."

In 2005, Callie Angell, director of the Warhol Film Project at the Whitney Museum, gave an interview to *New York* magazine that included a funny bit of trivia that was never previously noted: Warhol and Mekas made accidental appearances in the film. When reloading their camera, the men turned on the lights in Romney's office in order to properly set up their takes. But three times during the shoot, they began filming before turning the office lights off. As a result, their reflections can be glimpsed a few times in the office window.

"No one had ever mentioned that before," Angell said. "Probably no one ever had sat through the whole thing."

The Fat Spy
(1966, directed by Joseph Cates)

WHILE THIS FILM'S TITLE may suggest a spoof on the 007 genre, *The Fat Spy* is actually a spoof on the *Beach Party* flicks of the early 1960s. Indeed, there is very little spying going on here and the intrigue that shows up is closer to corporate espionage than secret agent derring-do. But there is a fat man in the film—actually, there are two of them, played by the same actor.

The eponymous girth belongs to Jack E. Leonard and you probably have never heard of him unless you were watching TV in the 1950s and 1960s. Leonard was a bombastic stand-up comic who specialized in put-down humor and Borscht Belt jokes. His brand of comedy was acceptable in five-minute appearances on Ed Sullivan's variety show, but he clearly wore out his welcome with an extended presence. *The Fat Spy* gave Leonard his first starring film role and, not surprisingly, his last.

The Fat Spy takes place in Florida, where a group of teenagers take a boat to a seemingly deserted island on a treasure hunt for the golden goodies buried by the Spanish conquistadors of the sixteenth century. Unbeknownst to them, the island is the property of the House of Wellington, a cosmetics conglomerate. Mr. Wellington (veteran character actor Brian Donlevy clearly reading his lines from cue cards) and his daughter Junior (Jayne Mansfield) receive word of the teenagers' presence from Irving (Leonard), a bumbling botanist on the House of Wellington staff and the caretaker/sole tenant on the island. Mr. Wellington fears the teenagers are after the legendary Fountain of Youth that can be found on the island, so Junior volunteers to fly her airplane to the island to keep an eye on the teenagers, and to keep an eye on Irving, whom she adores.

Meanwhile, the House of Wellington's smarmy marketing chief Herman, who is Irving's twin brother (also played by Leonard), is in cahoots with the company's corporate nemesis Camille Salamander (Phyllis Diller)—they are in love and both are eager to bring down the House of Wellington. Camille has a Sikh servant who loves to be whipped by his boss, and he is jealous that Herman has taken Camille's attentions from his daily whippings.

Meanwhile, the teenagers on the island sing, dance, make out, and look for the buried treasure. One of the teens, a boy named Dodo, meets a mermaid. He decides to leave his bipedal friends and walks into the waves when his fishy female friend calls for him. No one seems to miss Dodo after he departs.

The problem (or joy, depending on your taste) is that nothing in the film is intentionally funny. Diller and Leonard try to engage in insult joke one-upsmanship, but the efforts are dismal: She pats his considerable girth and comments about seeing an entire basketball team in one suit while he sings a song that compares kissing her to kissing Darryl F. Zanuck (*Huh?*). Leonard tries to engage in physical humor with shtick that includes pretending to play a telescope like it's a flute, balancing himself on a child's bicycle, and shaking his generous belly while surrounded by bikini girls. He is so wrong for big-screen stardom that it is impossible not to consider who thought it was a good idea to put him on camera. Mansfield tries to generate laughs with her dumb blonde shtick, but that stale joke was already ten years old by the time the film was made.

Director Joseph Cates (best known for producing the Oscar telecasts and 1980s bombshell Phoebe Cates) constantly elbows the audience with a skein of jokes designed to call attention to the silliness of the procedures: the chief teen couple are dubbed "Frankie and Nanette," the actors constantly look into the camera to comment on the action, thought balloons pop up on-screen, and inter-titles appear to speed along the zanier aspects of the plot.

The film also promised a wealth of sequels at its conclusion, but none of the potential follow-ups, like *The Son of the Fat Spy*, were ever made (thank you, God!).

Fear and Desire
(1953, directed by Stanley Kubrick)

IN 1953, a small and strange film called *Fear and Desire* premiered at New York's Guild Theater. It was the first feature directed by twenty-four-year-old Stanley Kubrick, a photographer who had previously created three short documentaries. Despite a great review from the *New York Times*, which hailed it as a "moody, often visually powerful study of subdued emotions," Kubrick was embarrassed by *Fear and Desire* and at one time was quoted as saying the film was just "a bumbling amateur exercise." Over the years, Kubrick tried to track down and buy up every known print of *Fear and Desire*. The film was never made available for commercial viewing until after Kubrick's death.

Did Kubrick have a reason for keeping *Fear and Desire* out of sight? Absolutely! This is perhaps the single worst debut feature helmed by an internationally acclaimed filmmaker.

Filmed in a California park on a thirty-three thousand dollar budget that Kubrick allegedly raised by hustling chess games in New York's Central Park, *Fear and Desire* uses a bizarre screenplay by first-time writer Howard Sackler (who would later find his stride with the prizewinning play *The Great White Hope*) to tell an allegory set in an unnamed country during an unnamed war. Four soldiers have survived a plane crash (we don't see the crash, but they talk about it for a few minutes to assure the audience why they are where they are). The men are six miles behind enemy lines and their only hope would be to build a raft in Huck Finn style and float down a river to their troops. However, two distractions get in the way: the arrival of a silent peasant girl, who the soldiers tie to a tree so she won't betray their presence, and the unexpected discovery of enemy headquarters, where a general can be spotted in the window.

One of the soldiers goes crazy (babbling about Shakespeare's *The Tempest*) and winds up killing the girl when she tries to escape and another goes crazy sailing alone on the raft to take on the enemy in single-handed Rambo style. The other two soldiers actually infiltrate enemy headquarters and kill the general and his top aide (played, inexplicably, by the same actors who play the soldiers who burst in with guns a-blazin').

Does any of this make sense? Of course not, and Kubrick clearly must have realized there were problems from day one. He tried to spruce up these shabby shenanigans with artistic camera angles, which resulted in having the film littered with a surplus of intense and frequently surreal close-ups. Sometimes the actors glare straight into the camera while conversing and in one crazy fight scene, fists come flying smack into the lens. The film's technical problems are also compounded by continuity mistakes (more than a few attempts at matching reaction shots find the actors looking in the wrong direction) and an unsuccessful dialogue track (the film was shot without sound and most of the post-dubbed dialogue comes from off-camera).

But even when the dialogue is in sync, it is intellectually out of sync with lines like "We have nothing to lose but our future," and "Who else but me is buried under the chain of everything I ever did?"

There is also the matter of Gerald Fried's wildly noisy musical score, which seems more appropriate for a Godzilla romp than for this tiny flick.

And yet, *Fear and Desire* is appealingly bad in the manner that Ed Wood's sci-fi anti-classics are fun to watch. The film is silly without being abhorrently stupid—it certainly isn't boring—and the earnestness of the young cast and crew is so obvious that you inevitably feel sorry for Kubrick and his colleagues for mucking up.

There is also the sheer pleasure of realizing that Kubrick, perhaps the ultimate perfectionist, was capable of making the most imperfect of movies.

Gamera
(1965, directed by Noriaki Yuasa)

DURING THE LATE 1950S and early 1960s, Japan's most popular exports didn't come from the realm of automobiles or electronics. Instead, the country shipped out a loony series of monster movies that captivated film lovers all over the world. The idea of seeing Tokyo destroyed by the likes of Godzilla, Rodan, and Mothra kept movie audiences enthralled for years and in their own weird way, these zany movies helped to reintegrate Japan into the world community following the difficult post-World War II years.

These zany anti-classics were produced by Toho Studios. Daiei, the rival film studio, thought it could do Toho one better by creating its own monster and thus was born the 1965 *Gamera*.

For those who don't know, the monster Gamera is a giant turtle. Obviously, turtles are not exactly scary creatures—in fact, they are rather cute, albeit in a lazy manner. So taking your average pond turtle and growing it hundreds of feet doesn't really make it threatening—it only makes it hundreds of feet out of proportion.

Unlike his fellow turtles, Gamera is bipedal. In fact, the creature looks like a man in a turtle suit, complete with long human limbs. Gamera also has a mouth full of teeth, plus two lower-jaw tusks and the ability to roar like a lion. When he is agitated, he can even breathe an atomic flame jet (similar to Godzilla, his cross-town rival). Even better, Gamera can tuck in his limbs and head and shoot jet-propelled flames that enable him to fly.

Gamera opens in the Arctic, which may not be the obvious location to root a movie about a giant turtle. An aerial duel between U.S. and Soviet jets causes a Soviet airplane carrying atomic weapons to crash into the ice. That creates a polar meltdown, which then releases Gamera from his icy tomb. But this should not be a huge surprise since the film informs us that the local Eskimos were versed in bizarre folktales of a giant turtle that used to terrorize the igloo crowd since time immemorial.

Gamera doesn't choose sides between the Americans and Ruskies; like any self-respecting Japanese movie monster, his goal is to destroy Tokyo. Thus he makes a sharp southwestern turn and heads toward Japan. Before hitting Tokyo, he makes a stop along the coastline to terrorize a coastal village. His boisterous behavior results in the destruction of a lighthouse, but Gamera shows uncommon good manners by rescuing a fat-faced boy named Toshio from the wreckage. Toshio, who ironically has a turtle fetish, thinks Gamera is ultra-cool.

Gamera eventually makes it to Tokyo and, not surprisingly, begins destroying buildings. A combination of nutty scientists and humorless army officers concoct a plan to dynamite Gamera, which results in having him knocked on his back. Turtles on their backs are supposedly helpless, but Gamera uses his ability to fly to lift off from that awkward situation. Eventually, the scientists and the soldiers cook up another plan that is designed to lure Gamera into a giant rocket. Once he is trapped inside, the rocket blasts off to Mars, thus saving the Earth while supposedly dooming Gamera to die on the distant red planet. Nice way to kill a monster, yes?

In talking about *Gamera*, there are actually three different movies: the original Japanese version, the Americanized version that was released as *Gammera the Invincible* (with an extra "m" in the title), and the 1980s updated version that kept the original Japanese footage, but added new Yankee-dubbed dialogue. Needless to say, this is all quite confusing when one considers the source material is just a dinky black-and-white feature made for what appears to be a few yen.

As a movie monster, Gamera maintained a fan base over the years. After his 1965 debut, the creature returned in a series of outrageous movies that were played completely for laughs. As you can see, you just can't keep a good turtle down!

The Giant Claw
(1957, directed by Fred F. Sears)

IN THE AFTERMATH OF WORLD WAR II, the B-movie orbit was awash with flicks involving ridiculously oversized creatures wreaking havoc on the world. Some of these films—most notably *Them!* (1954) and the Japanese-produced *Gojira* (1954, later imported to the United States as *Godzilla, King of the Monsters!*)—attempted to make a serious social statement with their tales of Nature gone horribly awry. For the most part, however, the majority of the productions within this warped genre were little more than endless variations on a simple horror/sci-fi concept.

While most of the supersized monster films are merely forgettable, this 1957 effort enjoys an infamous reputation for the sheer absurdity of the creature in question. If the plot is to be believed, a gigantic bird from some hitherto anti-matter galaxy has begun to endanger the skies over America. The scientists in the film theorize the bird comes from the year 17,000,000 B.C. and more than a few feathers get ruffled when it decides to take up residence atop various New York City skyscrapers.

All told, this is not such a crummy idea for a cheapo programmer. But things became utterly ridiculous when producer Sam Katzman found himself short of funds to bring this endeavor to life. Copious amounts of grainy stock footage were used for the aerial sequences, while the monster bird was little more than an awkward marionette that inspired more groans and laughs than screams. The website Shadow's B-Movie Graveyard describes the monster as if "a buzzard, a giraffe, and Marty Feldman got caught in Andre Delambre's teleportation device (from 1958's *The Fly*) and this was the end result."

Leading man Jeff Morrow, who spends his on-screen time battling this feathery foe, would later recall his personal horror at being associated with the finished product.

"We shot the film before we ever got a look at this monster that was supposed to be so terrifying," Morrow said. "The producers promised us the special effects would be first class… but the first time we actually got to see it was the night of the premiere. The audience couldn't stop laughing. We were up there on-screen looking like idiots, treating this silly buzzard like it was the scariest thing in the world…. I was never so embarrassed in my entire life."

Columbia Pictures acquired the film and promptly dumped this mess in theaters, earning a quick profit. Clearly, there *is* money to be found in bad films.

Gigli
(2003, directed by Martin Brest)

The Internet Movie Database sums up the plot of this film in this extraordinary sentence: "The violent story about how a criminal lesbian, a tough-guy hit-man with a heart of gold, and a retarded man came to be best friends through a hostage." Really, who would *not* want to see a film with this story, especially if it stars the hottest celebrity couple of the moment?

Well, that might be making *Gigli* seem a lot more interesting than it is. The film offers a wealth of cinematic clichés—the tough-but-tender mobster, the lovable mentally retarded adult, the hard-edged lesbian who secretly digs guys, the emotionally weak lesbian who tries to kill herself, and gangsters that sit around all day and order hits on their perceived enemies—yet it produces a deficit of credible entertainment.

What went wrong? For starters, the off-screen lovers Ben Affleck (as the hit man Gigli, which rhymes with "really") and Jennifer Lopez as the "criminal lesbian" (to use the Internet Movie Database's language) had no on-screen chemistry whatsoever. It didn't help that Affleck was basically retreading his *Chasing Amy* shtick as a guy who beds lesbians. However, Brest's screenplay made the character thoroughly unlikeable.

"Lemme tell you something," Affleck says to Lopez at one point. "In every relationship, there's a bull and a cow. It just so happens that in this relationship, right here with me and you, I'm the bull, you're the cow. All right?"

Even worse, Lopez was not even vaguely believable as a hit woman who babbles about "pussy power" while doing yoga exercises. "You know," Lopez says to Affleck. "I heard you were a bit of a fuck-up. But, frankly, I'm amazed at how much of a fuck-up you really are!"

Some distraction can be found with cameos by Al Pacino as a prosecutor, Christopher Walken as a detective, and Lainie Kazan as Affleck's overbearing mother. Justin Bartha made his feature film debut as the mentally challenged kidnap victim and he received the only positive buzz in an otherwise near-unanimous slam of negative reviews.

Gigli boasted a $75.6 million budget and little more than $7 million in box office returns. The film earned the unwanted distinction of being the first to sweep all the major Razzie Awards, including Best Picture, Director, Actor, Actress, and Screenplay. The resulting catastrophe helped to reconfigure the next Affleck-Lopez starring vehicle, Kevin Smith's *Jersey Girl*, which sought to distance itself from this flop by dropping almost all mention of Lopez from its marketing push.

The *Gigli* flop certainly contributed to the couple's break-up, but both stars managed to go on to the proverbial bigger and better in terms of their respective careers. More damaging was the impact to Brest's career; despite his box office success as director of such hits as *Beverly Hills Cop* (1984) and *Scent of a Woman* (1992), the one-two punch of Brest-directed expensive flops *Meet Joe Black* (1998) and *Gigli* effectively ended his Hollywood career. To date, he has yet to direct another picture.

Godzilla vs. Megalon
(1973, directed by Jun Fukuda)

BY THE TIME those sons of fun at Toho Studios got around to making *Godzilla vs. Megalon*, the imagination well for the Japanese monster genre had become bone dry. So did the budgets for these flicks. This film recycles several ideas from earlier films, not to mention the footage from the previous films, into yet another inane Godzilla-saves-the-Earth adventure.

This time, the enemies come from below the Pacific Ocean: a hitherto unknown population called the Seatopians are upset by the atomic testing of the nasty humans and they decide to punish their neighbors upstairs by having the insectoid creature Megalon attack Japan. The fact that the Japanese would be the last ones to be dropping H-bombs is lost on the Seatopians—when it comes to Earthlings, the Seatopians believe everyone looks alike.

To aid Megalon in his havoc, the Seatopians establish contact with their extraterrestrial pals the Nebulans to send the monster Gigan down to Earth. With a tag-team of Megalon and Gigan, the only hope to counter their destructive power is the Big G himself. Teaming up with Godzilla is Jet Jaguar, a human-sized robot that somehow has the power to grow fifty feet tall in order to participate in the mayhem of monoliths. It is a slam-bang smackdown event and the fate of the world (or at least Japan) is at stake.

Godzilla vs. Megalon was clearly designed for a kiddie audience, so any attempt at analysis by someone over the age of ten is futile. Unfortunately, the majority of filmgoers are over the age of ten and any adult sitting through this shabby monster epic cannot help but laugh at the idiotic plot and bargain-basement special effects.

There is a hint at a homosexual human subplot involving the good-looking inventor of the Jet Jaguar robot, who lives with his best friend (a good-looking racecar driver) in an ultra-modern (for 1973) house. The fact that these two very pretty guys don't have girlfriends or interest in girls might set off the gaydar of the homo-obsessed members in the audience, though, admittedly, gay activists have rarely tagged this series of films.

Godzilla vs. Megalon was a commercial flop in Japan, a rarity for the series, and it did not come to the United States until 1976 when a company called Cinema Shares International acquired the rights (and deleted three minutes of mildly offensive footage in order to secure a G rating). Cinema Shares International tried to piggyback on the excessive marketing for the Dino De Laurentiis remake of *King Kong* by literally aping that simian lollapalooza's marketing campaign: the U.S. ads for the film placed Godzilla and Megalon atop the twin towers of the World Trade Center, which King Kong climbed for the 1976 film version. (Strangely, the advertisements with the monsters on the World Trade Center rooftops have an unintentional poignancy in the post–9/11 world.)

American audiences followed the lead of their Japanese brethren and avoided *Godzilla vs. Megalon*. Logically, that would be the end of the story. Yet the film could not be kept down. It returned in 1977 when NBC, incredibly, gave it a primetime spot (albeit in a severely truncated format) with John Belushi in a Godzilla suit hosting the presentation. That was a ratings flop.

Toho would eventually reboot the Godzilla series with somewhat more serious productions. But *Godzilla vs. Megalon* still holds a most-favored status for movie lovers with a taste for overcooked Japanese cheese.

Goodbye, Norma Jean
(1976, directed by Larry Buchanan)

TEXAS FILMMAKER LARRY BUCHANAN has enjoyed a mild cult following for his bottom-of-the-barrel sci-fi flicks, including *The Eye Creatures* (1965), *Zontar: The Thing from Venus* (1966), and *Mars Needs Women* (1967). In 1976, Buchanan put aside his zipper-backed monsters and plastic flying saucers to present a biopic on one of the most vibrant personalities of the twentieth century, movie icon Marilyn Monroe.

Perhaps he should have stayed with the flying saucers. Critic Jake Cremins of the site Movie-Gurus.com captured the essence of the film in a single sentence: "In the annals of cinematic sleaze, *Goodbye, Norma Jean* will surely earn a special place as one of the most hideously depressing pieces of trash ever to be made by Larry Buchanan or anyone else."

Buchanan's film is a weirdly lurid and tastelessly fictionalized account of the young Norma Jean Baker's search for a niche in the Hollywood studio system. (Never mind that the film provides her with the mane of platinum blond hair that did not become her trademark until *after* she first appeared on-screen.) She barely survives living in a hostile foster home and her initial efforts to secure a life for herself result in a brutal rape by a highway patrolman. But when Norma Jean wins something called the Miss Whammo Ammo contest, she becomes convinced that she has what it takes to become a big-screen legend.

However, the film suggests that the future Marilyn Monroe's ascension to stardom had nothing to do with talent and everything to do with her willingness to be sexually assaulted by various producers, casting agents, photographers, and other studio fringe people. The number of attacks against Norma Jean is so frequent and Buchanan's staging of these sex crimes is so crude that the film becomes fascinating for the diversity of its misogynistic excesses.

Buchanan hoped to generate publicity by hosting a national talent contest to locate an unknown to play the young Marilyn Monroe. The contest's winner was a nonprofessional named Alexis Pederson, but she rejected the grand prize of the starring role after reading the script. Instead, Buchanan cast starlet Misty Rowe, who appeared as one of the decorative haystack cuties on the TV series *Hee Haw* and briefly played Maid Marian in the Mel Brooks sitcom flop *When Things Were Rotten*. Rowe seized the role as a chance of a lifetime, but delivered a truly bizarre performance that swung between the Monroe persona of the baby-voiced bombshell and a career-obsessed dynamo that openly and ferociously declared her self-worth and determination to succeed in the dirty and violent world of movies; it is a strange and often fascinating performance, but for all the wrong reasons.

Rowe would later be the focus of a *Playboy* photo shoot in which she re-created some of Monroe's celebrated poses. But the would-be star glumly acknowledged that she was stuck in a crummy film. "We had no lighting, poor makeup, little or no direction," she claimed.

Rowe's complaints were justified: Buchanan created *Goodbye, Norma Jean* on a meager budget of $130,000. And not unlike his other cheapo endeavors, it earned back a hefty profit. Buchanan created a sequel in 1989 which further desecrated Monroe's legacy.

The Green Cockatoo
(1937, directed by William Cameron Menzies)

IN EXPLAINING THE PRESENCE of the 1937 British B-movie *The Green Cockatoo* in the lineup of the 2005 New York Film Festival, the Film Society of Lincoln Center diplomatically referred to it as "an attempt by the British film industry to make an American-style gangster film," adding the end result is "an interesting curiosity."

That was an understatement of devastating proportions! *The Green Cockatoo* was nothing short of the unintentional comedy discovery of the festival—a film so wildly off-target and unaware of its very ridiculousness that it becomes irresistibly endearing.

The Green Cockatoo follows a young rural girl named Eileen (René Ray) on her first train trip to London. She's searching for a job, although it is not clear what kind of work she can do. She has the screwed-up luck of sharing her train compartment with a fat, excitable, wild-eyed kook (William Dewhurst, who is not billed in the credits). He fills her with warnings of wreckage and ruin if she should decide to stay in London. When Eileen innocently asks the nut where she should stay while in London, he harrumphs: "I cannot give you advice—I am a philosopher!" Huh???

As luck would have it, Eileen's train arrives in London just as petty thug Dave Connor (Robert Newton, one of British cinema's prime hams) is trying to escape from the mobster Terrell and his gang. Connor double-crossed Terrell by failing to fix a greyhound race and successfully betting on the winning pooch. Terrell and his gang (all two of them) corner Connor in the station and stab him. But the wound isn't fatal and Connor crosses paths with Eileen. He gallantly offers to carry her suitcase to the nearest hotel while he is visibly wobbly in his steps.

In her hotel room, Eileen finally notices that Connor is dying and he tells her to find his brother Jim at the Green Cockatoo nightclub, where she should tell him that Terrell is the killer. Eileen nobly takes Connor's switchblade from his jacket to cut open his clothing in order to help him breathe, but he abruptly drops dead. The chambermaid arrives with a pot of tea and sees the dead Connor and Eileen holding a knife. The chambermaid calls for the hotel manager, who calls for the police. Eileen flees into the night and, through good fortune, finds an inebriated cab driver that takes her on a wild zigzag ride through London to the nightclub run by Connor's brother.

Not only is Jim the owner of the Green Cockatoo, but he is also the floor show: he sings mawkish ballads, jokes with the boozing guests, and performs a tap dance number on a stage the size of a napkin. Jim is played by John Mills and he gives what is perhaps the most energetically miscast performance in movie history. Mills stands about five foot four and is blessed with one of the most distinguished voices in cinema, yet the film insists he is a two-fisted tough guy in the James Cagney/George Raft mold. When the going gets tough, he gets going, whether it's swinging a switchblade in a brawl with the sweep of Toscanini conducting a symphony, standing on his tiptoes to slug a taller opponent on the chin, or (in the ultimate act of hard-boiled he-manship) picking up the telephone to make threatening calls.

Mills is completely ludicrous to watch, but the tonic is hearing him try to talk the talk. When he claims his club "is knee-deep in coppers," or he advises a lethargic butler to "cut yourself a slice of sleep," or he boasts that he only wants brunettes and insists on "none of those dizzy blondes for me," the only possible reaction is laughter. He sounds like a member of the House of Lords who saw too many Cagney movies while downing a surplus amount of ale. It is no wonder René Ray looks at him and the whole film with perpetual bafflement—the poor lady probably could not understand how she wound up in this stew.

Anyway, Eileen and Jim wind up getting chased by Terrell's three-person gang and the London police force (which seems to consist of two fat men). The rest of the film consists of a brawl in an abandoned warehouse with a member of Terrell's gang, a pause for a coffee break from a sidewalk coffee vendor (whose customer base consists of two idiot Cockneys), a stop at a friend's country mansion, a trip to the mortuary to identify Jim's brother (remember him?), and a final showdown in Terrell's flat (Jim just walks in and punches everyone into submission). Then, rather abruptly, the film ends after sixty-five minutes right back in the same train compartment where the whole silly thing began.

For such a puny film, *The Green Cockatoo* actually has a lot of talent behind it. The story is inspired by a Graham Greene tale (I can't imagine how Greene reacted to the quasi-Warner Bros. gangster patter used here) and the flick was directed by, of all people, William Cameron Menzies. The celebrated American art director had just completed helming the British sci-fi epic *Things to Come* and, for no clear reason, took this little assignment. Menzies left England after directing this and returned to Hollywood to create the art direction for *Gone with the Wind* (talk about playing both ends of the spectrum!). There is also a sweeping and fairly overcooked music score by Miklós Rózsa, although its bombastic fury makes it seem more appropriate for a pirate epic instead of this rinky-dink exercise.

The Green Cockatoo was made by the British subsidiary of 20th Century Fox, but the studio did not release it. In fact, it sat on a British shelf for three years until it was screened. It turned up again over the years in England under different titles and finally showed up in America in 1947 via a fly-by-night distributor.

Hammersmith Is Out
(1972, directed by Peter Ustinov)

IF YOU'VE NEVER SEEN THIS FILM, find a spiritual channel of your choice and give thanks to the higher beings or deity therein. If you have seen it, however, come sit with me while I try to exorcise its residue from my soul.

Hammersmith Is Out takes the Faust legend and plops it into early 1970s America. It might have been considered a potential satire of American culture and priorities, except that it lacks any even vaguely sharp or witty observations on the topic. It could have been strictly a vanity show for its high-profile stars Richard Burton and Elizabeth Taylor, except that they barely seem to have any emotion to offer this inert mess.

It is possible this could have been seen as an act of alchemy by its director, British actor Peter Ustinov, with the hope that he could create a piece of cinematic gold from a screenplay that was pure lead. Unfortunately, that did not happen. Ustinov was a rather underrated director and he helmed a trio of notable films in the 1960s that rarely get considered today: *Romanoff and Juliet* (1961, based on his popular play), *Billy Budd* (1962), and *Lady L* (1965). These were all prestige films, framed for the highest common intellectual denominator. Viewed today, these films are vigorous and mature in their use of language and innovative in their visual presentation.

Hammersmith Is Out is another story. It is a crude, mindless, wretched waste of film that relies on scatological language and mildly offensive gestures to generate laughs. In regard to style, it has none. Had I not been aware in advance that Ustinov was the film's director, I could never have guessed he was calling the shots behind the camera.

Hammersmith Is Out focuses on dim bulb Billy Breedlove (Beau Bridges), a nose-picking good ol' boy that works as an orderly in a mental institution. He takes pleasure in harassing one of his colleagues, a bit of a sissy who occupies his spare time with needlepoint creations. Billy is genuinely intrigued by Hammersmith (Richard Burton), a bizarre maniac who is kept in a straightjacket in a padlocked cell separated from those of the other patients.

One night, Billy rides his motorcycle to a local diner and falls in love with the waitress Jimmie Jean Jackson (Elizabeth Taylor in a blond wig). After very small talk, they make love in the back room, where a sack of tomatoes is used as a makeshift mattress. Billy believes that Jimmie Jean is Ms. Right and they agree to elope.

But Billy decides to take Hammersmith along. Hammersmith makes strange, sinister promises to bring fame and fortune to Billy. Not being the brightest crayon in the box, Billy eagerly liberates Hammersmith.

At first, Hammersmith is able to keep his promise of providing high-ticket material belongings by viciously disposing of the original owners of the merchandise: the owner of a luxury car is stuffed in its trunk; the owner of a fine suit is stabbed in the gut; the owner of a profitable nightclub is pushed from a high window to his death, etc. Neither Billy nor Jimmie Jean are aware of how Hammersmith is able to provide these immediate riches and they savor the opportunity to enjoy newfound joy amidst the trappings of the entertainment world, the corporate suite, and the corridors of government power.

So what went wrong? For starters, Burton and Taylor clearly did not have their hearts in this project. Ustinov told Burton to go through the film without blinking— obviously to suggest the lunatic power of the Mephistophelean character. But Burton never bothered to put any life into his character, either—the solid gaze of his eyes was matched by the stolid nature of his presence. Rarely has pure evil ever been so enervated and the lack of menace makes Hammersmith a bore.

Likewise, Taylor is completely wrong as the dumb Texas waitress who gets swept up in the story. Despite a Dolly Parton–style wig and an on-again/off-again accent, you can't get around the fact you're watching Elizabeth Taylor (complete with movie-star tan and Cleopatra eye make-up) trying to be something she is not.

Beau Bridges tries to carry the film and he manages to get some genuine acting onto the screen. But he is undercut by a dull story and his character quickly becomes a hillbilly bore. Veteran actors George Raft and Leon Ames briefly turn up, but their presence is so mechanical that it is easy to assume someone wound them up like clockwork toys.

Ustinov is also in the film as the head of the mental hospital where Hammersmith was incarcerated. He does a bogus German accent and spends most of his time reacting to the stupidity around him. Had he played Hammersmith, one could imagine there would've been more vigor and imagination in the role. Ah well, it didn't quite happen and Ustinov would never direct another film after this tanked at the box office.

Still, as flops go, this one is fascinating for its riches of talent and poverty of results. Hammersmith should have stayed out of theaters!

Harvard Man
(2002, directed by James Toback)

LONG BEFORE ENJOYING cable TV stardom via *Entourage*, Adrian Grenier was the eponymous character of this off-the-wall flick. Grenier's Alan Jensen is a philosophy student and the star of the Harvard basketball team. Never mind that Grenier is too old and too short for the dimensions of this role; in fact, this miscasting is the least of the film's woes.

Alan seems to have everything: his own luxurious dorm room (no roomies in sight), a hot-hot-hot cheerleader girlfriend named Cindy Bandolini (Sarah Michelle Gellar), and another hot-hot-hot girlfriend who happens to be his philosophy professor (Joey Lauren Adams).

One day, Alan receives news that his parents in Kansas lost their home in a tornado and are now stuck in a Red Cross shelter. Alan flies home and locates his poor folks, who stupidly never bothered to insure their home against this possible calamity and, thus, are now completely destitute. However, Alan's parents blithely inform him that they will be fine and he should go back to Harvard and continue with his studies. Somehow or other, Alan determines that his parents need $100,000 to start life anew, so he jets back to Harvard and asks his gal-pal Cindy if her dad can loan him the money. Why Cindy's dad? Well, as convenience would have it, Cindy's dad is just the most important Mafia kingpin in the area and Alan assumes he is literally dripping with money to share.

With virtually no intense persuasion required, Cindy's dad happily agrees to give Alan the money as a gift, not as a loan. But Cindy decides to have a bit of fun: she informs Alan that he can only have the money if he throws an upcoming basketball game. Cindy plans to bet against Alan's team via her father's bookies (Eric Stoltz and Rebecca Gayheart). But unbeknownst to everyone, the bookies are actually agents in the Boston office of the FBI. Actually, they are the entire Boston office of the FBI—the movie's tight budget limits the number of on-screen agents to just this duo.

If this isn't bad enough, there is also an out-of-nowhere subplot where a classmate gives Alan three cubes of super-duper LSD. For no reason whatsoever, Alan decides to ingest all three cubes at once, setting him off on an acid trip that boosts his running skills to Road Runner-worthy speed. Alan races wildly through the streets of Cambridge while being chased by the FBI, his girlfriend, two goonish hit men sent by his girlfriend's father, his professor, the classmate who gave him the acid, and (in lieu of throwing in the kitchen sink) Al Franken, playing himself.

Harvard Man is such a frenetic mess that it often feels like a live-action Tex Avery cartoon, only without the carefully plotted humor. Characters jump out of windows, pull guns on each other, race about streets and hallways at supersonic speed, engage in frenetic sex at a moment's notice, and drive like maniacs with a death wish. Ah, but you really know it's just a movie when the drivers are able to find parking spaces in Boston without any problems!

The film also prefers old-fashioned stereotypes in lieu of well-written characters, serving up the lame images of vulgar Italian-American gangsters, oversexed African-American men, and modern women who talk tough, but whose defenses crumble with the first phallic poke to their nether regions. The only thing missing from *Harvard Man* is Harvard University, which had the good sense not to allow this shabby production anywhere near its campus.

Harvard Man also includes a brief but engaging performance by a Coca-Cola can, which enjoys significant prominence in a café exchange between Adams and Gayheart. The soda can is actually more alluring and gives a better performance than either actress and one should be genuinely rueful that more time was not devoted to its place in the plotline.

Head
(1968, directed by Bob Rafelson)

There are two musical sequences in the 1968 film *Head* which are among the most visually arresting concepts ever put on film. The first comes abruptly in the film's opening sequence, where the Monkees disrupt the dedication of a new bridge. Micky Dolenz, chased by his band mates, jumps from the bridge and falls in slow motion into a waterway that dissolves into psychedelic imagery. "The Porpoise Song," a trippy tune that floats with narcotized energy, pervades the soundtrack as a pair of pretty mermaids rescues Micky from the kaleidoscopic depths.

The second sequence features Davy Jones, without the other Monkees, performing "Daddy's Song," a bittersweet music hall-style ditty written by Harry Nilsson. Jones, assisted in an elaborate dance number by Toni Basil, sings and dances while the visual style keeps shifting—a black-clad Jones and Basil against a white background are interlaced with a white-clad Jones and Basil against a black background. It is a hypnotic gimmick that works remarkably well and Jones's excessively theatrical spin on the "Daddy's Song" lyrics suggests that his career could have gone far if he had stayed on the West End stage instead of venturing into the realm of bubble gum pop.

Sadly, those sequences are barely remembered today because *Head* is recalled as the Monkees' single disastrous adventure into feature films. After all, no one goes looking for great moments in flop films. The film's legendary failure has been blamed by Monkees fans on critics that dismissed the Monkees as lacking talent and Columbia Pictures' odd decision to promote the film without mentioning the presence of the Monkees as its stars. But, in truth, *Head* is an extremely mixed bag that tries too hard to be iconoclastic.

Basically a plotless revue of weird skits and silly sight gags with pauses for some tuneful interludes, the film took a gamble by seeking to elevate the Monkees from the level of tween novelty to a new level of hipster jokers. Its failure was not a lack of trying on the part of first-time director Bob Rafelson and creative collaborator Jack Nicholson (a year before his career turnaround in *Easy Rider*). Indeed, much of the film offers witty and pointed barbs at Hollywood clichés and conventions and a cheerful parade of unlikely self-deprecating stars (including Victor Mature, Annette Funicello, boxing champ Sonny Liston, and a wonderfully deadpan Frank Zappa) add a happy lunacy to the endeavor.

The problem, quite frankly, is the Monkees. Throughout the film, the lack of chemistry between the quartet's members is fairly obvious; it often seems like the foursome was only introduced to one another before the cameras began rolling. Dolenz and Jones clearly loved being on camera and they constantly (and often winningly) camera-hogged their scenes to the fullest. But their comrades Michael Nesmith and Peter Tork never seemed to be on the same energy level with them and the film had a lopsided clumsiness whenever all four were expected to interact. It is no surprise that the film's two standout numbers were the aforementioned Dolenz and Jones solo efforts and not a group interaction.

As for the music: well, some Monkees' fans insist that Nesmith's "Circle Sky" was among the band's finest, while "Diego Ditty-War Chant" offered a cogent self-satire of the Monkees' prefabricated sitcom roots. Eh, different strokes for different folks.

Ultimately, *Head* was a mess—an interesting and entertaining mess at times, but still a mess. The film has gained some degree of cred over the years based on nostalgia for the Monkees and the tie-dyed giddiness of the late 1960s. Of course, nostalgia can also diminish the severity of old failures and paint a deceptively pleasant memory over them that is at odds with the truth.

Health
(1979 directed by Robert Altman)

HEALTH (sometimes spelled *HealtH* and *H.E.A.L.T.H.*) came at an odd time in filmmaker Robert Altman's career. He hit a peak in 1975 with *Nashville*, which was one of the great artistic triumphs of the 1970s. But having peaked, Altman had nowhere to go but down and the remainder of the decade found him turning a skein of expensive flops: *Buffalo Bill and the Indians* (1976), *Three Women* (1977), *A Wedding* (1978), *A Perfect Couple* (1979), and *Quintet* (1979).

Health is a sloppy, sprawling would-be satire of the American political system except that it obscured its subject too effectively. Altman cloaked his political parody amid the hullabaloo of a health food industry convention which was in the process of electing its own president. There are two main candidates: an elderly incumbent (Lauren Bacall) and a verbose challenger (Glenda Jackson). Some critics saw these characters as distaff stand-ins for Dwight D. Eisenhower and Adlai Stevenson, but their personalities are so far removed from the well-known quirks of those 1950s icons that such a suggestion seems odd. Plus, there's an independent gadfly candidate (Paul Dooley) who buzzes about the convention trying to get attention for his campaign—and there was no 1950s version of such a presidential political candidate.

The real president (the White House variety) is represented here by a White House deputy staff advisor on health issues (Carol Burnett), who arrives at the convention to relay a message from the Commander in Chief. She is the ex-wife of the incumbent's chief political advisor (James Garner), who is also present.

The health food convention takes place at a Florida hotel, where a harried public relations manager (Alfre Woodard) is trying to keep all of the eccentric guests happy. There's also a backgammon hustler (Henry Gibson) who showed up to fleece some of the fitness nuts of their cash. And Dick Cavett is on hand to capture all of this for his TV talk show.

So what's the problem? For starters, Altman tries to use his *Nashville*-style of filmmaking in *Health* by having a tapestry of offbeat characters zigzagging through their colorful stories. In the course of *Health*, Lauren Bacall's character announces the secret to her good health is virginity—orgasms take months off your life. Paul Dooley mistakes Henry Gibson for a male prostitute. And poor Carol Burnett tries to get a laugh by screaming over the discovery of a dead body in a swimming pool while a man dressed like a tomato jumps into the swimming pool to save her.

The so-called Altmanesque school of filmmaking is in full throttle here, but it crashes almost immediately. Whereas *Nashville* was rich with a kaleidoscope of genuinely fascinating characters, *Health* is stuffed with one-dimensional, boring stereotypes that have little to offer in the way of genuine interest. Rarely have so many charismatic stars appeared on camera in such a dreary manner. In retrospect, it is fascinating that neither Altman nor his starry cast realized they were making a terrible blunder.

Health cost $6 million to produce, which was a lot of money back in 1979. Twentieth Century Fox delayed the film's release from Christmas 1979 to Easter 1980 and then put it on indefinite hold. Altman hosted a Los Angeles screening in September 1980 in order to pressure the studio to release the film, but the studio did not budge. Indeed, the studio's refusal to make the film available was without precedent—even the dreariest of A-list offerings wound up in theaters, if only for a brief spell.

Health was never shown publicly until April 1982 when a stand-alone limited release was arranged with New York's Film Forum, the major art house venue for the Big Apple. Vincent Canby, then chief critic of the *New York Times*, responded to this presentation by observing, "By all conventional standards, *Health* is, I suppose, a mess, but it is a glorious one in the recognizable manner of a major filmmaker who sometimes gets carried away—by his subject, by his own enthusiasms and those of his actors, and by the collaborative creative process he loves." Canby also hinted that the Reagan White House hated the movie, but it is not clear how or even why ol' Ronnie and his pals would even be interested in this enervated dud.

The failure of *Health* and Altman's 1980 musical *Popeye* all but killed his Hollywood career. He spent the 1980s and much of 1990s working on independent projects. And while his career enjoyed a resurrection in the late 1990s, the sickly *Health* still remains one of Altman's most elusive titles.

The Hottie & the Nottie
(2008, directed by Tom Putman)

FOR REASONS THAT WILL CERTAINLY BAFFLE future cultural historians, there was once a brief period in human history when Paris Hilton was among the most famous people on the planet. Her celebrity was not based on any particular achievement or beloved talent— she was just famous for being famous.

Cashing in on Hilton's notoriety proved to be something of a challenge. A reality television show *The Simple Life* initially created a ratings hit for her that led to quickie books and cameo appearances in a few movies. In an attempt to secure even greater fame and fortune, Hilton agreed to star in and serve as executive producer for a comedy called *The Hottie & the Nottie*. It was, ultimately, not a wise decision.

In concept, the film was basically a standard-issue comedy with Hilton as the California "hottie" who enjoys overheated male attention whenever she steps outside. A classmate from her school years is eager to become part of her life, but she will only tolerate him if he can find a boyfriend for her supremely unattractive and horrendously smelly best friend (played by Christine Lakin, who is made up like a Neanderthal). The quick-thinking would-be Lothario gets a part-time male model and aspiring dentist to deal with the "Nottie," but the miracle of dental surgery and aggressive makeup skills turns the one-time "Nottie" into a rival "hottie."

While the film toils in gross-out comedy at the expense of its "Nottie," whose physical ugliness is taken beyond weak farce into harsh and mean-spirited cruelty, the real shock comes in watching Hilton try to act. While even Hilton would admit she is not in the same league as Meryl Streep, even the three-time Oscar winner would be hard-pressed to make sense of impossible lines such as "Our bodies are earth suits, vessels to help us pass from this planet to the next" and "A life without orgasms is like a world without flowers." Yet Hilton's vapid emoting (and, quite frankly, annoying voice) work against whatever physical attractiveness she is trying to exploit. And filling the movie with pathetic men who become obsessed with her (including, of all things, an albino stalker) makes the film nearly impossible to endure.

The puerile and superficial nature of the comedy, coupled with the media's distaste for Hilton, created an immediate offense among critics. Nathan Lee of *The Village Voice* slammed the film as "crass, shrill, disingenuous, tawdry, mean-spirited, vulgar, idiotic, boring, slapdash, half-assed, and very, very unfunny." Sam Adams, writing for the *Los Angeles Times*, observed, "It's not like Paris Hilton to rise above her material, but *The Hottie & the Nottie* sinks so low that all she has to do is stand upright."

Produced on a $9 million budget, *The Hottie & the Nottie* earned a pathetic $27,696 on its opening weekend in February 2008. The film quickly disappeared from sight, although it was remembered by many critics for their worst-of-the-year lists and by the funsters behind the Razzie Awards.

Hilton also faded from view, at least on the big screen. Outside of a supporting role in the offbeat 2008 musical *Repo! The Genetic Opera*, she has stayed away from films and concentrated more on keeping her star afloat via reality television and personal appearances at celebrity events. To date, few people rue her absence from cinematic projects.

Hugo the Hippo
(1975, directed by William Feigenbaum and József Gémes)

HUGO THE HIPPO takes place on the East African island of Zanzibar. In the English-dubbed version of this Hungarian production, narrator Burl Ives thoughtfully informs us how Zanzibar is a "lazy" and "sleepy" place—and if you're starting to feel a bit queasy with the possibility of racist content, you're not being overly sensitive. In fact, this is one of the most astonishingly insensitive animated feature films of all time.

The film's opening sequence features a group of African laborers standing mid-waist in a shallow port loading the contents of a freighter. The Zanzibar laborers are attacked by a school of sharks wearing biker regalia. Along the shoreline comes Zanzibar's minister of finance, the evil Aban-Khan. He is given a bitchy voice by *Hollywood Squares* icon Paul Lynde. When viewing the shark attack, he demands to know, "In the name of Allah, what are you doing?" Hearing Paul Lynde wrap his sing-song, mincing voice around the word "Allah" is both hilarious and vaguely blasphemous.

The shark crisis dominates a cabinet meeting run by Zanzibar's sultan, a fat man in a turban who keeps company with a wise pet cheetah. British actor Robert Morley voices the sultan and you may be wondering about Zanzibar given the weird mix of accents. The sultan consults with his hippie wizard, who is not very clever beyond a few card tricks and the accidental transformation of the sultan into a large boar. For some reason, it is determined that the port will be safe with the addition of a hippo squadron in the waters. Don't ask why, given that the average hippo exists far from the average shark and the two are not natural enemies.

A dozen hippos are captured and dumped in the harbor, including the eponymous Hugo. He's a baby hippo, the son of the hippo king. The hippo brigade is successful in eliminating the sharks (one hippo punches a shark so hard that only the fish's sharp teeth remain floating about). The

Zanzibar people respond initially with generous treatment, but soon forget the good hippo deeds and the creatures are left to starve. One night, they rampage through Zanzibar in search of food and destroy a clove farm. Aban-Khan, who hates hippos, arranges to kill the creatures and one night, he assassinates nearly all of them (the killings are shown by having lightning bolts destroying hippo-shaped clouds followed by Hugo's discovery of dead hippos lying on the floor of the bay).

Little Hugo finds himself on the run without shelter or friends. The local jungle animals are oddly hostile and prevent him from accessing food; at one point, two nasty apes pick up a cabbage and use it to play basketball. A young boy named Jorma befriends Hugo and gives him food and attention. But the bond between a boy and his hippo is soon tested by angry, hippo-hating adults who go to great lengths to kill Hugo.

For a G-rated film aimed at kids, *Hugo the Hippo* is a surprisingly mean and violent affair. Hugo is constantly being harassed and endangered, either by being deprived of food, being pelted with stones, or being attacked with swords and guns. Even the obligatory happy ending is strangely incomplete—the Zanzibar people never express any remorse for the hippo slaughter or the violence that they bring against Hugo.

But the most disturbing thing about the film is not its substance, but its style. It seems the Hungarian animators watched *Yellow Submarine* and *Fantastic Planet* a few too many times and felt they could meet or exceed the psychedelic imagery of those classics. Thus, a big yellow sun with a scowling face illuminates Zanzibar and its skies are filled with purple seagulls that fly about in a state of mild confusion. A giant blue-and-purple butterfly also turns up to ferry Jorma and Hugo on a trip into a parallel universe of planets made of fruits and vegetables.

If that's not crazy enough, there's the pop music soundtrack featuring Marie Osmond and her kid brother, Jimmy. Marie barely pays attention to the songs (she's not a little bit country, just a little bit bored), but screechy little Jimmy somehow thinks he's Ethel Merman and belts out lyrics with show-stopping panache. However, those lyrics leave a lot to be desired. Consider this hippo description: "He walks like an elephant, / He swims like a whale. / His head's like a pail, it's pathetic, / Oh, plainly his tail's unaesthetic." Burl Ives also gets to sing a happy tune about Hugo's near-starvation, exclaiming how he's so famished that he could "eat the ox in oxygen."

Needless to say, if you have very naughty children in need of severe punishment, this film is the perfect tool for such torture!

The Human Centipede (First Sequence)
(2009, directed by Tom Six)

THE FIRST RULE of exploitation cinema is an old carny axiom: Sell the sizzle, not the steak. And in the case of this horror film created by Dutch filmmaker Tom Six, there was plenty of sizzle thanks to the most atrociously outrageous concept in movie history.

Set in an isolated part of Germany, the film follows the unfortunate journey of two dimwitted young American women whose automobile breaks down on an unfamiliar road. They arrive at the house of an extremely mad surgeon, who happens to have his own medical facility in his basement. How the crackpot doctor managed to lug all of his medical equipment into his private residence without raising a sniff of suspicion is never explained.

Needless to say, the surgeon takes a liking to the ladies and promptly drugs and imprisons them. They find themselves trapped alongside a very loud (and non-English-speaking) Japanese man and the surgeon provides a PowerPoint lecture outlining their fate: they are to be surgically joined in a mouth-to-anus procedure that will create a "human centipede."

Yeah, never mind that this "centipede" will be dozens of limbs short of its insect inspiration. The surgeon, working by himself at an extraordinary speed, assembles his bizarre work in his quasi-hospital basement. But in order to maintain his captives in a position of permanent subservience, the surgeon severs the ligaments in their knees, thus preventing them from being able to stand.

Yes, this is a grotesque but fascinating idea for a torture story. But this is also where *The Human Centipede (First Sequence)* makes a big mistake. The genuine terror is in waiting for the medical captives to be surgically disfigured into this abhorrent creation. Once the "centipede" is assembled, however, it doesn't really do anything. The mad doctor tries to teach his sewn-together captives to move as a single unit, but they are so slow and cumbersome that they barely make progress. And the Japanese man who serves as the "head" of the centipede doesn't stop yelling throughout his imprisonment, annoying his captor (not to mention the viewer).

Eventually, a pair of police detectives shows up in search of the missing Americans. They become suspicious of the mad doctor, resulting in an enervated duel while the "centipede" attempts to escape by crawling up a staircase. To Six's credit, the film has a downbeat ending, but it actually inspires more giggles than gasps, if only for the sheer absurdity of the situation.

Six, to his credit, keeps the gore level low—no mean feat considering the plot. The actual surgery used to create the monstrous concept of the human centipede is barely shown and once the centipede is assembled, Six cheats the audience by using bandages and careful camera angles to avoid highlighting the detailed results of this surgical procedure.

Most critics were not fooled. Roger Ebert, noting the wildly exploitative nature of the film's marketing, wrote that Six and his backers "deliberately intended to inspire incredulity, nausea, and hopefully outrage." Ebert declined to assign the film a star rating in his noncommittal review. "The star rating system is unsuited to this film," he wrote. "Is the movie good? Is it bad? Does it matter? It is what it is and occupies a world where the stars don't shine."

Well, the stars shined on the film's release, earning it a notorious cult movie reputation and a tidy profit. But audiences weren't fooled twice, as Six discovered when his 2011 sequel generated relatively little attention and even less financial return.

If Footmen Tire You, What Will Horses Do?
(1971, directed by Ron Ormond)

THIS 1971 BAPTIST propaganda film represents the unlikely collaboration of Rev. Estus W. Pirkle, a Mississippi preacher who had a minor following thanks to mail-order sales of audiotaped sermons, and Ron Ormond, a Grade Z filmmaker who gave the world such nonsense as *The Monster and the Stripper* (aka *The Exotic Ones*) and *Girl from Tobacco Row*. Ormond came to Rev. Pirkle's peculiar theology after being born again, although his embrace of faith did not include an upgrade in his filmmaking skills. With this film, Ormond simply replaced the buxom starlets of his older flicks with fat redneck broads in polyester dresses shouting "Praise Jesus!" while keeping the rickety and incompetent trademarks of his cinematic style.

If Footmen Tire You, What Will Horses Do? feels like it was created by people with attention deficit disorder—three completely unrelated stories ping-pong back and forth around the screen in a bewildering manner. The first is a straightforward and humorless sermon by Rev. Pirkle on how early 1970s America was pushing God away and embracing the foundations of moral ruin. While citing some obvious troubling developments of that era, including the rise in urban crime and violent unrest on college campuses, Rev. Pirkle goes even further in spotting sin. As the good pastor pontificates, drive-in theaters are "spawning houses for sex," Saturday morning TV cartoons "teach our children crime, sex, and murder," and dancing... oh, don't get him started on that!

The second story line involves Rev. Pirkle's prediction that the Soviet Union would successfully conquer America within twenty-four months unless there is a mass revival to embrace his version of Christianity. The film includes sequences of what a Soviet-run America would look like:

Stalin look-alikes dressed in tsarist military uniforms riding on horses and terrorizing God-fearing hicks, forcing them to work from five A.M. to eight P.M. 363 days a year; the two free days are for praising the Marxist way of life.

The movie goes out of its way to imagine the depravity of Soviet-style repression. There are multiple shots of dead bodies lying in bullet-riddled wreckage (although the blood on the victims looks conspicuously like cherry sauce dribbled about pell-mell). And those who don't give in to the party line that "Communism is Good! Christianity is Stupidity!" face intense torture. In one amazing scene, a Soviet soldier (with a fairly strong Mississippi drawl, but never mind) grabs a small boy and shoves a bamboo shaft into his ears so he will not be able to ever hear the Word of God again. The boy emerges from the assault with giant sticks hanging out of both his ears, at which point he begins to vomit profusely into the camera.

The third story involves Judy, the local slut who shows up late in the sermon wearing a psychedelic miniskirt that seems more appropriate for *Laugh-In* than a Rev. Pirkle revival meeting. Judy is initially bored with the sermon, but as the film progresses, she inexplicably gets caught up in the Commie chatter and then begins experiencing flashbacks about her own naughty behavior (which includes hanging out with a shady guy in a cheap cafe and drinking beer out of a Styrofoam cup). Judy then recalls her poor old fat and sloppy Momma, who succumbed to a heart attack because Judy would not accept Jesus and forsake her bad behavior. Judy begins hallucinating about her Momma's funeral and how she cried uncontrollably over the open coffin (but if she looked up, she would have seen Momma visibly breathing when she was supposed to be stone-cold dead). Judy makes a spectacle of herself when she goes to the altar, kneels in her miniskirt (giving a nice view of the gates of heaven to those in the front pew), and announces that Jesus is her savior and Rev. Pirkle is her middleman to the Man from Galilee.

Will somebody give me an *Amen*?

In Old Chicago
(1937, directed by Henry King)

THEY DON'T MAKE FILMS like this 1937 extravaganza from 20th Century Fox, and that might be a good thing! An epic inspired by the Great Chicago Fire of 1871, this production obliterated historical accuracy in pursuit of cheap laughs, mild sex appeal, and enough corn to keep the nation's ethanol plants at full production for a year.

In Old Chicago focuses on the exploits of the O'Leary family—and yes, the pyromaniac cow is part of the clan. But most of the attention belongs to the wildly mismatched sons of the rambunctious Irish widow Molly O'Leary, who runs a "French laundry" in a sprawling urban neighborhood known as "The Patch." Oldest son Dion (Tyrone Power) is the handsome rogue who parlays his gambling fortune into a bold grab for neighborhood power. Middle son Jack (Don Ameche) is the good-natured but somewhat bumbling lawyer who never quite comes out ahead in his cases. And youngest lad Bob (Tom Brown) stays close to home and marries the blond Swedish maid who helps Mrs. O'Leary with her work.

Oh, there's also a leggy showgirl (Alice Faye) whose brassy exterior hides (what else?) a heart of gold. She falls for Dion despite his scamp behavior and they team up to muscle out crime boss Gil Warren (Brian Donlevy). Alas, Mrs. O'Leary does not want Dion to be involved with a showgirl, which creates ill will between mother and son.

Dion orchestrates an elaborate bit of election manipulation to get his brother Jack elected mayor, but Jack abruptly takes on his own reformist agenda that targets Dion's slimy business operations. Dion and Jack get into a fistfight over this. Fortunately, Mrs. O'Leary's cow knocks over a lamp that starts a wee blaze that destroys the entire city while reuniting the fractured O'Leary clan except for Mayor Jack, who is assassinated by Gil Warren's gang while the city burns down.

Although the film begins by giving thanks to the Chicago Historical Society for its help in the production, the only accurate thing about this film is that there is a city called Chicago. Beyond that, it's every man, woman, and cow for themselves. The real Mrs. O'Leary was named Catherine, not Molly, and she was not a widow. (In its opening sequence, the film has poor Mr. O'Leary dying in a covered wagon accident!) Nor was her cow responsible in any way for the fire—the man who first blamed the bovine, *Chicago Tribune* reporter Michael Ahern, admitted he made up the tale.

Nor did Mrs. O'Leary's son grow up to be mayor. During the 1871 fire, Chicago's mayor was Roswell B. Mason and he was not assassinated.

But even if one forgives the historical errors, the film's acting is an utter nightmare. Tyrone Power was in his matinee idol phase at the time, so his performance was strictly all about grinning widely and posing stiffly in tightly tailored clothing. (There is a brief glimpse of him with his shirt unbuttoned.) Alice Faye was a charming singer, a not-so-graceful dancer, and a terrible dramatic actress; she's great during the film's several musical numbers, but less than heavenly when the music stops. Don Ameche smiles a lot, then frowns a lot, and then dies in a melodramatic tumble. Alice Brady somehow won an Academy Award for her Mrs. O'Leary despite a blatantly bogus brogue and some of the broadest Irish stereotyping this side of *The Quiet Man* (complete with vigorous consumption of huge mugs of beer).

There are a few distractions here to keep the viewer amused: the great African-American character actress Madame Sul-Te-Wan steals her few scenes as Alice Faye's daffy maid while poor misshapen Rondo Hatton lurks about several scenes as a neighborhood thug. And yes, the fire sequence is impressive for 1937-level special effects, though it is hard to imagine today's CGI-weary audiences being dazzled by the trickery.

In Old Chicago cost $2 million to produce, which was a grand sum in those days. Fortunately for the studio, it was a major box office hit and even snagged a Best Picture Oscar nomination. Go figure!

Inchon
(1982, directed by Terence Young)

This film always suffered from a crummy reputation because of who produced it: the Unification Church, also known as the Moonies (named in honor of Sun Myung Moon, the religion's founder). Back in the late 1970s and early 1980s, there was an extraordinary level of fear and apprehension regarding the Moonies, who were seen as being among the most disreputable cults ever to corrupt the God-fearing world. When *Inchon* was first released, the mania against the Moonies was at its highest pitch. Many people believed the film was being used to recruit new members to the faith while others feared the box office profits would go to enrich the church coffers. In 1982, it was impossible to judge the film on its own merits because of the controversy surrounding its backers.

Inchon focuses on the start of the Korean War. North Korean tanks and hordes of running soldiers break across the 38th parallel into South Korea. This creates a mass exodus of South Korean villagers, who race to safety in the capital city of Seoul. Also in the exodus is Jacqueline Bisset, playing the wife of a U.S. major. She happens to be in a village at the 38th parallel, where she is negotiating to purchase antique furniture. With her posh British accent and skin-tight, cleavage-bearing outfit, Bisset is not your stereotypical U.S. Army officer's wife. Nonetheless, she isn't fond of the North Koreans and she gets into her chauffeured limousine en route to Seoul.

Meanwhile, her husband (played by Ben Gazzara) is in Seoul, trying to wrap up a love affair with a lovely young Korean lady. Her father, played by the great Japanese samurai star Toshirô Mifune (who is clearly not comfortable with his English dialogue), seems to approve of the affair. News of the invasion is relayed to the major, who manages to hook up with an African-American sidekick/sergeant (Richard Roundtree). They head north, looking for Jacqueline Bisset.

Over in Tokyo, a group of cynical journalists led by David Janssen (wearing an anachronistic late 1970s haircut) is waiting for a press conference to be held by General Douglas MacArthur. A new journalist joins their group—a somewhat campy music critic who is inexplicably assigned to cover serious news out of Tokyo. That role went to (of all people) Rex Reed, whose campy line readings suggest that he is playing himself (but not playing *with* himself, as he did in *Myra Breckinridge*).

But the general never shows up—he's at home in Tokyo with his wife and dog. The general, by the way, is played by Laurence Olivier wearing one of the most unconvincing makeup jobs ever slapped on a prime thespian. MacArthur happily agrees with his wife that he is the only person who can save South Korea from the Commie invaders.

In case you were wondering where the Koreans are in this story, there are two subplots. One involves a young couple whose wedding plans are torn asunder when they are separated during the chaos of the invasion. The other involves a group of Korean kids who climb into Jacqueline Bisset's car—she winds up driving them to safety (her chauffeur gets killed during the North Korean attack, so she has to hit the gas).

Will Ben Gazzara and Richard Roundtree find Jacqueline Bisset? Will Jacqueline Bisset get those Korean kids to safety? Will David Janssen stop cracking bad jokes at MacArthur's expense? Will Laurence Olivier convince anyone he is really General MacArthur? Will Toshirô Mifune master English? Will Rex Reed stop acting like Rex Reed? And will anyone do something about those annoying North Koreans?

If you manage to stay all the way to the closing credits of *Inchon*, you will find the answers. And if you don't... well, there are ninety-nine other films in this book to explore!

The Iron Petticoat
(1956, directed by Ralph Thomas)

THE IRON PETTICOAT was an independent British-based production about a female captain in the Soviet Air Force who flies her jet fighter to a U.S. base in Germany. She announces that her defection is based on her anger for being overlooked for a promotion. However, she remains a full-blooded Communist and has nothing but disdain for the West. A major in the U.S. Air Force is dispatched to help win her into the U.S. political camp, but since he is trying to woo a British heiress, he conspires to take the Soviet defector to London. However, the Soviet government is wise to these actions and they attempt to kidnap their pilot and return her to Moscow. By this time, however, the Soviet lady pilot and her U.S. major fall in love.

If all of this sounds familiar, that is because it is. Similar stories about Commie gals embracing Western ideals and guys were used by Greta Garbo in *Ninotchka* (1939) and Hedy Lamarr in *Comrade X* (1940). Josef von Sternberg's *Jet Pilot* had a very similar plot involving a defecting Soviet female pilot; that film had its highly publicized production in 1950, but producer Howard Hughes delayed its release until 1957. On stage, Cole Porter created *Silk Stockings*, a musical version of *Ninotchka*, which had its New York premiere in 1955.

As *The Iron Petticoat* was originally envisioned, Katharine Hepburn was cast as the defecting Soviet Air Force pilot and Cary Grant would be the U.S. Air Force officer. Grant, however, declined the role. For reasons that still remain unclear, the role was given to Bob Hope, who immediately insisted upon top billing (Hepburn obliged without incident).

But the Hope-Hepburn combination never sparked. Director Ralph Thomas would later remark to writer Charles Higham: "Really, they were playing in two different pictures. She was a mistress of light, sophisticated romantic comedy, he was much broader, and eventually, I didn't so much direct the picture as watch them in action."

What went wrong? For starters, Hope arrived at the London set with an entourage of gag writers. He viewed Ben Hecht's screenplay and decided that it needed to be funnier—with Hope's character getting most of the laughs via his trademark snappy wisecracks. For example, when Hepburn tells Hope that he has an odd face, he responds: "It came with the body—it's a set." (And that is one of the film's funnier lines!) Topical political humor and an obligatory in-joke reference to Bing Crosby were also part of the mix.

It is not certain if Hope's gag writers also pushed for *The Iron Petticoat* as a title. The project was originally called *Not For Money*. One source claims that Hope wanted to quit the film before shooting began out of a fear that he would be upstaged by Hepburn. Hope's actions were not lost on Hepburn, who later told biographer Charlotte Chandler that the funnyman's surplus of jokes "overwhelmed my character. I didn't care. I wished he would have overwhelmed me right out of the film."

Still, Hepburn made no attempt to save the film. In fact, she was totally lost as the Soviet flier. Her version of a broad Russian accent was disastrous and it didn't help that she was yelling her lines in the film's first half, though in the film's second half, she seems to visibly lose interest in the contrived plot of counterespionage and mistaken identities to the point of briefly dropping her Russian accent in a couple of dialogue exchanges. While Hope was playing his comfortable screen persona, Hepburn came across like a complete maniac.

Metro-Goldwyn-Mayer picked up *The Iron Petticoat* for U.S. theatrical release and the studio planned a major promotional campaign; Hope even dropped word of the film during a guest appearance on *I Love Lucy*. But its opening in New York in December 1956 was a fiasco. Bosley Crowther, the *New York Times'* film critic, dismissed the unlikely teaming of Hope and Hepburn as "something grotesque" and other critics were equally hostile.

The Iron Petticoat had a scant release and was quickly withdrawn from theaters. Curiously, MGM would go back to the same formula of the Ruskie woman and American male charmer in 1957 with its film version of Cole Porter's *Silk Stockings*.

In an odd postscript, *The Iron Petticoat* was banned in Rangoon, the capital of Burma, in 1958 following a protest from the Soviet Embassy that the film was a slur against Russian women. Burma has since become Myanmar, though whether the film is still banned there is not clear.

The Jazz Singer
(1980, directed by Richard Fleischer)

THE LANDMARK 1927 Al Jolson feature *The Jazz Singer* ushered in the era of talking pictures. The 1980 remake had a significantly less important impact on motion picture history, except perhaps to reconfirm the belief that classic films should never be remade.

In some ways, the film's title is a misnomer because nobody actually performs jazz tunes. The production was anchored on Neil Diamond making his acting debut, but the performer offered a soundtrack of light rock tunes.

This version of *The Jazz Singer* kept the basic foundation of the Jolson original—the struggle between an aspiring Jewish-American performer and his strict Old World father, a synagogue cantor—but it made several changes that derailed the film's logic. The biggest problem is reconfiguring the central character (played by Diamond) as a married man who is already established as a synagogue cantor, but who secretly writes tunes for an African-American singing group. When one of the group's members is unable to appear at a gig, Diamond's character puts on blackface to take his place—whether this is a tribute to Jolson or just a bad racist joke is unclear.

Unlike the Jolson character, who struggles between a religious tradition that has yet to consume him and the lure of show business glitz, Diamond's character abruptly (and, in truth, arrogantly) forsakes his responsibilities to his wife and synagogue and heads to Los Angeles, where he achieves fame virtually overnight while divorcing his wife and impregnating the shiksa talent scout (Lucie Arnaz) who helps launch his career.

Clearly, there is plenty of angst to spare. But the pain created by Diamond's actions is turned into unintentional comedy by Laurence Olivier's performance as his father. Using a thick Yiddish accent that sounds like a tribute to Mel Brooks's 2,000 Year Old Man, Olivier roars through the film with such extraordinary overacting that the film veers into the realm of unintentional comedy when he rends his garments and shrieks, "I haf no zon!" Olivier would later express regret for his participation in *The Jazz Singer*, sheepishly acknowledging that he only did the film in order to grab a generous paycheck.

As an actor, Diamond was unable to offer the level of charisma and kinetic energy displayed by Jolson in the 1927 original—or, for that matter, the goofy charm that Danny Thomas and Jerry Lewis provided in their respective 1952 film and 1959 television remakes of the property. Several critics noted that Diamond had problems making eye contact with his fellow actors. As a result, it was difficult to sympathize with his character's tumult when he gave the impression of being surly.

To his credit, Diamond offered a strong soundtrack that compensated for his dramatic deficit. The hit songs "America," "Hello Again," and "Love on the Rocks" came from this film and the soundtrack album became a top-selling achievement in Diamond's career.

Although Diamond was nominated for the Golden Globe Award for Best Actor in a Comedy or Musical, he achieved some degree of immortality by snagging the Worst Actor honors in the first Razzie Award ceremony. The star avoided film acting for three decades, returning before the cameras to play himself in the 2001 comedy *Saving Silverman*, which involved the misadventures of the members of a Neil Diamond tribute band.

Joan Rivers: A Piece of Work
(2010, directed by Ricki Stern and Annie Sundberg)

THIS IS ONE OF THE MOST DEPRESSING movies ever made—so depressing that it makes the Ingmar Bergman canon look like a Jim Carrey laughfest. But its miserable mood is fascinating because it is supposed to be a documentary about comedian Joan Rivers.

So why is this film so depressing? Well, there are two reasons. First, Rivers comes across as a raging monster of self-pity. Wallowing in insecurity and trumpeting a constant fear of losing her star standing, she seems utterly unaware that she has been among the most successful stand-up performers of our times. With a lavish Manhattan apartment, a limousine and chauffeur, and a staff whose livelihood is supported by her star power, the septuagenarian Rivers is among the very few comedians who has been able to stay on camera, snag book deals, and fill large venues for more than four decades.

However, this is not good enough. Rivers bitches and moans that Kathy Griffin gets to play the prestige houses in Las Vegas while she has to make do with a casino in Wisconsin—never mind that she arrives there via a private corporate jet and leaves with a performance fee that most people are unable to earn in the course of a year.

Throughout the film, Rivers endlessly snarls that the entertainment media's critics never supported her dramatic endeavors. Indeed, she claims bitterly that they spent years refusing to take her seriously as an actress.

Oh? It seems that both the star and the creators of this documentary forgot about her well-regarded dramatic supporting role in the 1968 film *The Swimmer* starring Burt Lancaster, her well-received 1988 performance in Neil Simon's New York stage production of *Broadway Bound*, and the Tony Award and Drama Desk nominations she received for her

1994 play *Sally Marr and Her Escorts*. Of course, if she wanted critical acclaim, perhaps Rivers should have actually bothered to pursue a real acting career instead of doing stand-up comedy, shilling cheap jewelry, and making fun of well-dressed stars at award ceremonies.

Second, this is one of the sloppiest researched biographical documentaries of all time. Among the items missing from her life story: Rivers's first marriage to James Sanger (which lasted six months in the 1950s), her brief attempt at Off-Broadway theater in the early 1960s (including a role in the play *Seawood* opposite another unknown named Barbra Streisand), her successful books and comedy albums, her many years of highly rated guest appearances on variety programs and game shows, and her work as the director and writer of the critically slammed, but commercially successful 1978 comedy film *Rabbit Test*.

There is a good deal of attention devoted to Rivers's controversial failure as the host of a late-night talk show and the disastrous falling out she had with her one-time mentor, Johnny Carson, when she dared to go up against him in the ratings. But the film never bothers to recall that she bounced back from that failure with a successful five-year run as the host of a daytime talk show, for which she snagged a Daytime Emmy Award.

Instead, Rivers is constantly whining about a lifelong fear of being considered an irrelevant has-been. Huh? Then I guess feature-length nonfiction films are produced about irrelevant has-beens?

Seriously, I wish I had Rivers's money and career! If that happened, you'd see a biographic documentary about a damn happy person, not some chronic whiner who is crying all the way to the bank.

King Lear
(1987, directed by Jean-Luc Godard)

BACK IN 1985, Israeli-born B-movie producer Menahem Golan surprised the Cannes Film Festival with his announcement that he signed Jean-Luc Godard to direct a new production of *King Lear*. The colorful partnership signing ceremony took place at a café table with the French filmmaker affirming his participation in an agreement written out on a napkin.

Godard and Golan decided to hire Norman Mailer to write the screenplay. Mailer presented a vision of a dying Mafia chieftain named Don Learo, but the controversial novelist complicated matters by insisting that he play the role. Mailer's daughter, actress Kate Mailer, was cast as Learo's daughter Cordelia. But the Mailers had a falling out with Godard and departed the production after one day of shooting and Burgess Meredith and Molly Ringwald (at her teen queen peak) were brought in as the replacement Learo and Cordelia.

However, anyone looking for Shakespeare in Godard's *King Lear* will be disappointed. Oh, there is a Shakespeare: William Shakespeare Junior the Fifth, played by theater director Peter Sellars. This Shakespeare is a somber, spiky-haired chap who lives in a period right after the Chernobyl nuclear meltdown, where the world was contaminated in a manner that somehow resulted in the loss of all works of culture. Never mind that people remained healthy or that food and water remained safe—incredibly, the works of Shakespeare's famous ancestor mysteriously vanished from all of the world's bookcases thanks to the Ukrainian nuclear mishap.

Thus, Shakespeare follows Learo and his daughter around a posh resort, eavesdropping as they converse in bits and pieces of what might be the dialogue of *King Lear*. Shakespeare also makes the acquaintance of

Professor Pluggy, a cigar-smoking eccentric wearing a wild wig consisting of electric cords and colored wires. Pluggy, played by Godard, is also obsessed with making photocopies of his hand.

Throughout the film, obscure intertitles flash across the screen. "A Picture Shot in the Back," "Fear and Loathing," "No Thing," "An Approach," and "A Clearing" (which is also presented as "A cLEARing") are repeated while absurd sound effects, including screeching seagulls and honking horns, fill the soundtrack.

While some Shakespearean dialogue is used (mostly in theatrical recitations by Meredith), there are also chunks of the Mailer screenplay, which makes campy references to old-time gangsters. At one point, the action moves outside with scenes of Ringwald showering her attention on a white horse.

Somehow or other, Shakespeare winds up in a film editing studio run by Mr. Alien, played by Woody Allen. The bespectacled actor-director looks glum as he edits film using safety pins and a needle and thread. Shakespeare falls into a large pile of unspooled film while Mr. Alien (clearly reading from a cue card) offers a couple of lines from Shakespeare. And then *King Lear* stops without actually ending.

If anyone other than Godard created *King Lear*, the film would never have found its way into a movie projector. But the fact that Godard is responsible does not bring any value to the production. While it would be foolish to expect a completely faithful adaptation from Godard, there is no pleasure in being tricked into thinking that this vague, obscure, annoying, cacophonous wreck of a film is anything but a joke being played by a self-indulgent filmmaker.

Even Woody Allen realized the film was a disaster during the shooting of his brief scene. "It was one of the most foolish experiences I've ever had," he recalled in an interview. "I'd be amazed if I was anything but consummately insipid."

Allen never saw the finished film, but he was hardly alone. The film had a scant release and remains one of Godard's least-seen works. Indeed, the film's lack of resonance was so strong that a young Quentin Tarantino attempted to inflate his early career credentials by falsely claiming he had a role in the production—in Tarantino's mind, so few people saw the film that no one would challenge his claim of being a cast member.

Klezmer on Fish Street
(2004, directed by Yale Strom)

DOCUMENTARY FILMMAKER Yale Strom has helmed a number of fine films, including *The Last Klezmer: Leopold Kozlowski, His Life and Music* (which was shortlisted for the Best Documentary Academy Award), *Carpati: 50 Miles, 50 Years,* and *L'Chayim, Comrade Stalin.* This effort, however, sadly represents one of the most incompetent nonfiction films of all time—indeed, it is so badly made that it is almost fascinating to watch in order to learn how *not* to produce a nonfiction film.

According to the press notes accompanying its initial release, *Klezmer on Fish Street* alleges there is "a resurgence of interest in Jewish culture" in today's Poland. The notion behind this grand statement is a thriving so-called Holocaust tourist trade, including a *Schindler's List*–inspired tour of the Nazi death camps and the now-extinct Jewish neighborhoods of Poland's major cities.

The film also insists that there is a strong Polish interest in klezmer, a distinctly Russian-Polish music identified with the Jewish culture of this part of the world; allegedly, many non-Jewish Polish musicians are playing this music to sold-out concert engagements throughout the country.

Unfortunately, what is depicted on-screen completely contradicts such notions. Open-air performances of klezmer music in Poland by a group of young American visitors are received by Polish pedestrians with gazes ranging from studied indifference to outright contempt. An evening street celebration following the Jewish Sabbath brings out both the local police (who are visibly unhappy with the event) and insults from local Poles suggesting the celebrants should go to Israel.

As for historic preservation, the film shows that although few vestiges of pre-1939 Jewish culture have been preserved, spray-painted swastikas turn up on more than one occasion. As for the Holocaust tourist trade, it seems to thrive on cheap souvenirs depicting traditional Jewish art and a few restaurants that may not even be kosher. (The film doesn't even bother to ask how the food is prepared.)

Klezmer on Fish Street is a hodgepodge of vague and unfinished thoughts, bizarre comments, and some of the most amateurish production values in a supposedly professional production. In one hilarious moment, an Israeli tourist is being interviewed when a man walks in front of him and stops in the center of the camera's focus. The screen is filled with a huge close-up of the intruder's ear while the Israeli tourist continues to bloviate from behind the man's head.

Elsewhere in the film are whooshes of wind blowing heavily into a microphone, soundtrack levels rising and falling willy-nilly, poorly blocked close-ups which make the interview subjects look comic, night-time footage so dark that you cannot tell who is speaking, and selections of Yiddish songs presented without English subtitles.

There is also an inane historian who claims klezmer music is the "soundtrack for the Jewish experience"—a fact that will come as news to the millions of Jewish people of Sephardic heritage. This individual also worries about the Gentile takeover of klezmer with this immortal concern: "The issue is not that a white boy can play the blues, but can a goy play the Jews?" Oy vey!

The cruelest blow of them all, however, is the fact that this movie had a theatrical distributor and played in theaters. Granted, the film made a near-zero impression—it only grossed $5,734 in box office receipts in its opening, while *New York Times* critic Elvis Mitchell dismissed it by saying the film looked "as if someone turned a vacation tape into a documentary, or rather tried to." But in view of the scores of extraordinary documentaries that never find an audience, the ability of this little mess to get on a screen is the cinematic equivalent of rubbing kosher salt in a wound.

The Last of the Secret Agents?
(1966, directed by Norman Abbott)

THE ONLY FILM FEATURING the boisterous comedy duo of Marty Allen and Steve Rossi was supposed to be a parody of the James Bond genre—a major mistake since 007 was a sly parody of espionage thrillers. It also didn't help that director Norman Abbott (Bud Abbott's nephew) and writer Mel Tolkin (one of Sid Caesar's gagmen from *Your Show of Shows*) had no idea how to create a feature-length motion picture. Both men were grounded in TV production, where a half-hour episode was standard issue. The challenge of filling a movie was too much for them, resulting in a production that lurched erratically from scene to scene. (Both men concentrated on writing and directing for TV after the film was released.)

The Last of the Secret Agents? finds Allen and Rossi as Americans barely eking out a living in Paris by doing odd jobs. And they inevitably get fired due to Allen's incompetence. Their latest gig, moving a piano, results in the instrument being smashed to splinters. The one respite from their shaky existence is a nightclub where Rossi's girlfriend is the venue's owner, thus enabling them to eat and drink for free. Nancy Sinatra, who attempts to merge with her character via a wildly bogus French accent, plays the girlfriend. (She also sings the film's title song.) Her father is played by Lou Jacobi, also doing an egregious Gallic dialect. They are the only people in the film trying to sound French—which is interesting considering the film takes place in France.

Anyway, agents from GGI (Good Guys Incorporated), a global secret agent network, abduct Allen and Rossi. It seems the men who hired them to move that piano were art smugglers working for criminal operation THEM (the acronym is not defined). The pair is recruited to go back and keep tabs on these characters to determine where the stolen art is being stored. To communicate with the GGI leaders, they are given an umbrella that doubles as a walkie-talkie and lethal weapon.

And that's about all there is to *The Last of the Secret Agents?* The remainder of the film has Allen and Rossi chasing the art smugglers or the smugglers chasing them as they attempt to steal the Venus de Milo. Since the movie is a low-budget affair, the chasing is limited to slamming doors and running down hallways.

For the most part, the comic action centers around Marty Allen trying to be funny. Some of his shtick includes waving at a white-bearded man and yelling "Merry Christmas," rolling his eyes while blowing into a trumpet, wearing baggy pajamas while combing his wacky hair over his eyes, and having a fold-up bed fall on his head. Steve Rossi manages to get a song in during a party sequence, but he mostly looks on as his zany partner runs amok.

The *New York Times* barely acknowledged the film's existence and unfairly dismissed Allen and Rossi as lacking talent. "Neither the script, the director, nor Mr. Allen and Mr. Rossi display the kind of mad comic invention, which can sometimes run smoothly," said the newspaper's by-line-free review. "Not even the kids will get a ride out of this one."

Lost Horizon
(1973, directed by Charles Jarrott)

LOST HORIZON, James Hilton's utopian novel, was first adapted for the screen in 1937 by Frank Capra. By 1973, Columbia Pictures still owned the screen rights to the Hilton text and decided to adapt it into a musical. This was not a bad idea since musicals were still a potent force at the box office: *Fiddler on the Roof, Cabaret, 1776,* and various Disney endeavors were packing cinemas at that time.

All of the right players were brought in: producer Ross Hunter, who flew *Airport* to major box office success; director Charles Jarrott, who helmed the acclaimed dramas *Anne of the Thousand Days* and *Mary, Queen of Scots*; Oscar-nominated screenwriter Larry Kramer penned the script; legendary choreographer Hermes Pan tied his shoelaces and prepared the dance numbers; and chart-topping tunesmiths Burt Bacharach and Hal David handled the musical score. For the on-screen talent, Peter Finch, Michael York, Liv Ullmann, George Kennedy, Sally Kellerman, Olivia Hussey, Charles Boyer, and John Gielgud were all signed up.

Okay, that's where the film made its first boo-boo—the main cast was noticeably shy of musical stars. Even when the stars agreed to have their songs dubbed by professional singers (Finch, Ullmann, and Hussey were covered in this manner), they couldn't quite master the process of lip-synchronization. Peter Finch got off somewhat lucky—most of his songs were shot as internal monologues with the Australian star looking around pensively while the soundtrack filled with his dubbed singing voice played.

Liv Ullmann, in a 2001 interview with the British newspaper *The Guardian*, recalled her unlikely involvement in the production with good humor: "Well, I knew that I couldn't dance and I couldn't sing… I did say that to them and they said, 'Oh, it doesn't matter, you're so sweet and so charming, we'll work around it.' So somebody sang my voice and then I danced, and that looked kind of stiff and strange, but what I said was true. It was my first time in Hollywood and I believed everything they said, and they said every woman in Hollywood wants to do your part in *Lost Horizon*, and I believed that, too. I lived in this incredible house with this swimming pool and my friends came over, and the bathroom in the house was like, like this whole room! It was fantastic! Give that to any thirty-one-year-old from Norway and they will think that it's the greatest time in their life."

She may have had the time of her life, but audiences watching her performance as a free-spirited teacher romping about a quasi-Himalayan playland with a troop of bratty kids were left puzzled. Even if Ullmann was no rival to Julie Andrews, the Bacharach-David score was strangely banal and forgettable. But even then, there was another piece to the puzzle: *Lost Horizon* did not offer its first musical number until forty minutes into the movie. And then the songs did not seem to stop.

Actually, the film has one genuine musical performer: Bobby Van, who plays a nightclub entertainer that is brought to Shangri-La along with a motley collection of Americans and Britons. Van's obnoxious personality is highlighted with the ridiculous song "Question Me An Answer," where he celebrates stupidity before Ullmann's class. Van does a mild soft-shoe routine and ends his number by tap-dancing off a bridge into a shallow creek.

The musical numbers in *Lost Horizon* created much derision when the film was first released. A paean to family values called "Living Together, Growing Together" (performed by Japanese-American actor James Shigeta in his most substantial role since the 1961 musical *Flower Drum Song*) was particularly knocked for its simplistic lyrics: "Start with a man and you have one / Add on a woman and then there's two / Add on a child and what have you got? / You've got more than three, you have what they call a family." (Clearly, Rosie O'Donnell didn't live in Shangri-La.) The film also offered a "fertility dance" sequence with musclemen in thongs scampering about to music. That sequence, along with twenty-three minutes of songs, created so much unintentional laughter in preview screenings that the film's editors worked overtime to carve out the ultra-silly footage.

Before *Lost Horizon* opened, the film was pegged as a prestige production. Its Hollywood premiere attracted movie royalty and even Governor Ronald Reagan returned to his Tinseltown roots for the event. In London, the film was selected for the annual Royal Command Performance.

But then *Lost Horizon* opened and the savage reviews destroyed the film's credibility. Wise and witty critics ranging from Pauline Kael to Judith Crist to William Wolf tore the film apart with extraordinary verbiage. Even Bette Midler got into the act, quipping in her divine style: "I never miss a Liv Ullmann musical."

I must admit that my favorite pan of *Lost Horizon* belonged to my mother, who took the eight-year-old version of yours truly to see the film at the UA Valentine Theatre in the Bronx. Said my Ma, "I felt like dancing out of the theater!"

The Maltese Bippy
(1969, directed by Norman Panama)

THE COMEDY TEAM of Dan Rowan and Dick Martin first paired in 1952, but for many years, A-list stardom eluded them. Their careers were marked with many false starts, including a low-budget 1958 film called *Once Upon a Horse*, and the duo never really hit pay dirt until the 1968 premiere of their TV series *Rowan & Martin's Laugh-In*. The show's irreverent mix of slapstick skits, loony sight gags, hipster comedy songs, and pointed comments at then-relevant political issues helped to shake American television out of blandness and into a new state of hipster humor.

The ratings success of the TV program tempted Metro-Goldwyn-Mayer to push the team forward into a feature film. However, no one from the *Laugh-In* cast was invited to join them. Even worse, it was decided to reconfigure the team's established persona (Rowan's debonair straight man and Martin's appealing bubblehead) into new on-screen characters: Rowan was given a Bud Abbott fast-talking schemer part while Martin absorbed a Lou Costello-style frenzied schnook who winds up in the middle of the mayhem.

The film was called *The Maltese Bippy*. The title is a riff on *The Maltese Falcon* and the imaginary word "bippy," which was one of the team's popular catchphrases (specifically: "You bet your bippy!"). However, the film has no connection with *The Maltese Falcon* or anything even vaguely Maltese and no one trotted out their bippy.

In this production, Rowan and Martin are filmmakers shooting their latest endeavor, *Lunar Lust*, in a crummy Manhattan office. Rowan is the film's director, Martin is cast as the overly romantic astronaut, and buxom starlet Pamela Rodgers (who would later join the *Laugh-In* cast) is the extraterrestrial queen who knows nothing about the Earth habit of kissing.

However, a landlord demanding payment on unpaid rent interrupts the proceedings and the film is shut down.

The men pack up their belongings in a moving truck and go to Martin's creepy old home in the Flushing section of Queens, New York. The house is next to a cemetery, where the discovery of a dead body (not shown on-screen) brings around police investigators (including a young Robert Reed). Martin lives in the house with a wisecracking housekeeper (Mildred Natwick) and a young blond college student (Carol Lynley) who is renting a room. Next door, an equally creepy house is home to a pair of Hungarian siblings (Fritz Weaver and Julie Newmar) and their zaftig housekeeper (Eddra Gale). The latter has few lines and serves no purpose except to be the recipient of wisecracks about her weight.

For no clear reason, Martin has found himself howling at odd moments. His psychiatrist believes he is turning into a werewolf while the Hungarians next door confide that they are actually three-hundred-year-old werewolves. Martin is aghast, but Rowan thinks he can make a variety show act using the werewolves. However, the blond student helps Martin learn that the Hungarians and the psychiatrist are trying to drive him insane so they can locate a valuable jewel hidden in the house.

Does any of this sound funny? If you're not laughing, you're not alone. *The Maltese Bippy* is the rarest of birds: a comedy film that does not contain one single humorous moment. In fact, the film's utter lack of mirth actually becomes fascinating in a sick way—it is impossible to watch it unfold without wondering how it could possibly get worse.

And it gets worse and worse with each new reel. From the miscasting of Rowan and Martin in Abbott and Costello roles to the dust-covered haunted house clichés to Norman Panama's dreary direction, *The Maltese Bippy* is a weird experience.

Despite an unusually loud promotional campaign, audiences stayed away from the film. A planned second vehicle for Rowan and Martin, tentatively titled *The Money Game*, was scrapped and no other studio wanted to gamble on the duo after this film flopped. They never made another movie, although *Laugh-In* remained a high-rated TV series through 1973.

Mame
(1974, directed by Gene Saks)

WHEN *PAPER* MAGAZINE film critic Dennis Dermody was asked to name the scariest film of all time, he did not choose a horror flick or a thriller. Instead, he picked a musical starring one of the most beloved entertainers of the twentieth century.

"Lucille Ball wearing that awful mask and singing 'We Need a Little Christmas' in the 1974 film version of *Mame* is the most frightening experience I've ever had while watching a film," said Dermody in an interview with the *Hartford Courant*. "Really, it is the most terrifying thing ever put on screen."

Indeed, Dermody is not exaggerating. This film version of Jerry Herman's hit Broadway musical is notorious for being one of the most spectacular misfires of the 1970s. And the fault, sadly, lies in the tragic miscasting of its central player.

Mame opened on Broadway in 1966 with Angela Lansbury in the starring role. Warner Bros. bought the film rights in 1968, which seemed rather curious because the source material for *Mame*—the Patrick Dennis novel *Auntie Mame* and a subsequent Broadway adaptation starring Rosalind Russell—had already been made into a classic 1958 film with Russell brilliantly reprising her stage role. Trying to overcome the legacy of that film was a tall order.

Herman had reportedly held out hope for Judy Garland to star in the film version—the legendary star's poor health prevented her from acting in the role on stage—but Garland passed away in 1969. The most logical choice for the title role would have been Lansbury, but Warner Bros. was lukewarm to her potential commercial appeal. Although she had been in films since the mid-1940s and was a three-time Oscar nominee, Lansbury's film work was mostly in supporting roles and the studio executives were uncertain if she could carry a film on her own star power. But this was strange since Lansbury scored a box office hit as the star of the 1971 Disney musical fantasy *Bedknobs and Broomsticks*. Alas, it wasn't good enough for Warner Bros.

Instead, the studio turned to Lucille Ball, who was primarily a TV star and had not been on the big screen since 1968. Ball's ex-husband Desi Arnaz, on whom she still relied for advice after their divorce a decade earlier, tried to convince her not to take the role. Ball, who saw *Mame* in a Los Angeles-based stage production, felt that she could pull off the role and was eager to exorcise her "Lucy" persona with a new role.

From the beginning, *Mame* was a troubled production. Filming was to begin in early 1972 under the direction of George Cukor, but it was postponed after Ball broke her leg in a skiing accident. The delay forced Cukor to drop out and be replaced by Gene Saks, who directed the Broadway production of *Mame* and also helmed the popular film versions of *The Odd Couple* and *Cactus Flower*. Madeline Kahn was signed for the supporting role of Mame's secretary, Agnes Gooch, but Ball was uncomfortable with Kahn's approach to comedy and successfully petitioned to have her removed and replaced with Jane Connell, who played the part on Broadway. Ball was clearly less threatened by Connell, who was mostly unknown to film audiences whereas Kahn was beginning to gain a reputation for her unique comic style.

Additional casting discomfort arose in filling the part of the rambunctious stage diva Vera Charles. Ball's longtime TV sidekick Vivian Vance was eager for the role, but the studio feared that people would expect a big-screen version of *I Love Lucy*. Incredibly, Bette Davis publicly campaigned for the role (it is unclear why she was not considered). Saks ultimately chose his then-wife Beatrice Arthur, who played the role in the original Broadway production. Arthur was already famous for her role on the TV series *Maude*, but her role in *Mame* was relatively small and Ball was not uncomfortable with her presence.

Ultimately, *Mame* could not move beyond the mistake of having Ball at the heart of the film. At age sixty-two, she was at least fifteen years too old to play Mame Dennis. An elaborate makeup and wig regimen could not create the illusion of a youthful Ball and cinematographer Philip H. Lathrop didn't help matters by shooting his star through special lens filters that made her close-ups look slightly blurry. Indeed, the contrast between Ball's soft-focus presentation and the 20/20 clarity of her costars gave the impression of a film that constantly dipped in and out of focus.

Then there was the problem of Ball's singing voice. Ball's less-than-melodious vocalizing was a running gag on her various TV series and her only previous musical film, the 1943 *Du Barry Was a Lady*, was released with another woman dubbing her songs. Ball starred in the 1960 Broadway musical *Wildcat* and she earned praise for introducing the showstopper "Hey Look Me Over," but she was not up to the physical challenges of the role and the show closed after 171 performances.

Ball, to her credit, worked very hard with Jerry Herman in an extensive series of vocal rehearsals and seriously studied her dance moves with Oscar-winning choreographer Onna White. Unfortunately, her singing remained inadequate and her dancing betrayed a lack of grace. Yet Ball stubbornly refused to have her songs dubbed—the studio was forced to piece together different lines from multiple takes in order to create vocalizing that had some semblance of proper pitch—and she insisted on being part of the film's choreographed sequences.

Despite her intentions, Ball could not escape the "Lucy" persona that people expected from her. Even Vincent Canby of the *New York Times* could not divorce Ball from her TV creation. "When the character of Lucy, an inspired slapstick performer, coincides with that of Auntie Mame, the Big-Town sophisticate, *Mame* is marvelous," he wrote in his review. "I think of Lucy's turning a Georgia fox hunt into a gigantic shambles, or of her bringing the curtain down on a New Haven first-night when, as a budding actress, she falls off a huge cardboard moon."

And that's where the film failed. The film really wasn't *Mame*, but an extended *Lucy*-style episode with the star going about her trademark clowning in a variety of wigs and elaborate costumes. Sadly, the star was too old for such romping and ill-equipped for the musical interludes that peppered the film.

When *Mame* was completed, Warner Bros. realized it had a problem. The studio had initially planned the film as its 1973 Christmas release, but abruptly rescheduled it for a 1974 Easter unveiling. The critics, who sensed something was not right, eagerly awaited the film's unveiling and their reviews reflected an uncommon cruelty.

Paul D. Zimmerman of *Newsweek* was particularly vituperative. "There she stands, her aging face practically a blur in the protective gauze of softer-than-soft focus, her eyes misting, her remarkably well-kept figure gift-wrapped in the fashions of the twenties, looking alternately like any one of the seven deadly sins and a decorator wing chair," he wrote.

Stanley Kauffmann of *The New Republic* went further, condemning Ball as being "too old, too stringy in the legs, too basso in the voice, and too creaky in the joints."

The film left a sour residue on the talent involved. Saks would not be trusted to direct another film until *Brighton Beach Memoirs* in 1986. Paul Zindel, the Pulitzer Prize-winning writer who authored the screenplay, stayed away from film assignments until *Maria's Lovers* in 1984. And Ball, angry and hurt at the critics' insults, refused to make another theatrical film. Instead, she concentrated the remainder of her career on television, where audiences never fell out of love with "Lucy."

Manos: The Hands of Fate
(1966, directed by Hal Warren)

WHAT DO YOU GET when you give a Texas fertilizer salesman $19,000 and a 16mm camera? The answer is one of the most bizarre endeavors ever put before an audience—a production of such staggering incoherence and mind-boggling incompetence that the film's many fans claim it deserves the designation of being the worst movie ever made.

The fertilizer salesman in question was Harold P. Warren, also known as Hal Warren, and his unlikely place in movie history came via a bet with writer Stirling Silliphant in an El Paso, Texas, coffee house. Silliphant was in the city for a location shoot on the TV show *Route 66* and Warren managed to snag a walk-on bit. In conversing with Silliphant, Warren boasted that he would be able to make his own film, which was no mean feat considering he had zero experience behind the camera.

And the camera that Warren finally got behind helped to make his first film memorable (if only for the wrong reasons). Warren used an old 16mm Bell & Howell camera that needed to be wound by hand in order to shoot footage. Thus, he was only able to shoot takes lasting thirty seconds at a time. The camera's primitive condition also prevented Warren from achieving proper sound recording, thus requiring that all dialogue and effects be added in the post-production process. Warren raised $19,000 to finance his project, which he dubbed *The Lodge of Sins*, and recruited performers from local theater groups to appear as his stars.

Somehow along the way, Warren's vivid self-confidence and inefficient talent parted company. The resulting work, which was retitled Manos: The Hands of Fate, became a masterwork of sloppy, inane, and bewildering filmmaking.

Chris Heller of NPR probably defines *Manos* best. "*Manos* is entirely inexplicable," says Heller. "There's a satyr-like man named Torgo whose backward knees are themselves worn backward, a variety of Satanic rituals with little or no connection to the movie's goings-on, and a young couple that, for reasons unclear, spends the whole of *Manos* necking in a 1963 Triumph Spitfire. Allegedly, it's a movie about a family that gets lost on vacation, stumbles upon an old house in the middle of nowhere, then spends eternity as the mind slaves of some creep named The Master. But it's unfair—it's *inappropriate*—to accuse *Manos* of following any real plot at all."

What *Manos* lacks in plot, it makes up for in extraordinary distractions. Warren shot many of his exterior scenes at night, but the use of bright lights to illuminate his scenes attracted swarms of moths that found their way into the finished film. The opening sequence involving the lost family driving down unfamiliar roads dragged on endlessly with little dialogue—Warren had originally planned to run the opening titles over this extended sequence, but neglected to do so.

And the costume design for Torgo has become something of a mini-legend: in Warren's mind, the character's oversized knees belonged to a satyr with goat legs. But Warren lacked the skill and funds to bring his satyr to life and his screenplay made no overt mention of Torgo being a satyr. Thus, the character hobbled along (his footwear clearly visible) with ridiculously large knees.

Warren initially believed he created a serious film and orchestrated an elaborate premiere in El Paso. Alas, the initial screening for local dignitaries turned into a fiasco with some audience members laughing and hissing while throwing objects at the screen. Warren and his cast members, who arrived at the screening with pride in their work, sneaked away before the closing credits rolled.

Amazingly, Warren managed to get a regional distributor called Emerson Releasing Corporation to secure a few drive-in bookings for *Manos* in Texas and New Mexico; no reviews of the film were published during these brief exhibitions.

After its brief drive-in run, *Manos* was quickly forgotten. Because Warren neglected to register a copyright for the production, the film wound up in a catalog of public domain titles that was made available for local television stations. But on the fateful night of January 30, 1993, *Manos* came into its own when it was highlighted as the final feature presentation on Comedy Central's cult show *Mystery Science Theater 3000*.

Mike Nelson, the head writer for *MST3K*, told *Entertainment Weekly* that *Manos* stood out from the scores of silly and wretched films featured on the program. "We started watching it, and had never seen anything like that," Nelson recalled. "We kept saying to ourselves, 'There is no way we can do this movie, it is just too bizarre.' But we finally decided, 'No, we must bring this to the world.'"

Although *MST3K* unreeled scores of wretched and silly films, *Manos* was the one that seemed to click with audiences. It has the distinction of holding an unprecedented zero percent rating on Rotten Tomatoes and voters on the Internet Movie Database designated it as the worst film of all time. It also inspired three different stage musical parodies and a documentary called *Hotel Torgo*.

In 2011, the original 16mm print was discovered by Ben Solovey, a Florida State University film school graduate, who decided it was his mission in life to digitally restore *Manos*. But even Solovey acknowledged in an NPR interview that he was not giving great art to future generations: "It feels like you're watching a film from another planet," he said.

As for the film's fertilizer salesman creator, Warren never made another movie. His attempt to become a novelist with a book called *Satan Rides a Bike* ended in frustration when publishers rejected his work. He died in 1985, unknown to the wider cinematic world.

The Merchant of Venice
(2004, directed by Michael Radford)

ONCE UPON A TIME, Al Pacino was among the most talented and imaginative actors to grace the screen. By 2004, however, he seemed content to follow the late-career example of his *Godfather* costar Marlon Brando and use the motion picture medium to make a public fool of himself.

And what a fool he became! Pacino's performance as Shylock in *The Merchant of Venice* is astonishing and for all the wrong reasons. The great actor is completely unable to grasp the distinct cadences of Shakespeare's text and he tries to hide his shortcomings by stretching his lines to the fraying point. Each sentence is delivered in a weirdly elliptical, singsong manner that is spiced by a faint Yiddish accent. If you can imagine Yoda imitating Jackie Mason, you'll have an idea of Pacino's speech pattern.

On several occasions, Pacino abruptly launches into his *Scent of a Woman* persona and begins bellowing like a crazed moose. In these moments, Pacino reverts to his natural Bronx diction; thus, Shylock petitions the court with the demand "I crave da law!"

But beyond the spectacle of Pacino's miscasting, *The Merchant of Venice* has plenty of inanities to amuse the puzzled viewer. Director Michael Radford seems to have forgotten that most of Shakespeare's text is actually a romantic comedy. But rather than offer wry laughs, Radford opts for clumsy ethnic humor with Portia's suitors (the African chieftain seeking Portia's hand and his entourage represent the worst on-screen minstrelsy this side of *The Green Pastures*) or sour snarky sneers (Portia's strident inquisition about the absent ring should be reason enough for Bassanio to seek a divorce lawyer).

Unlike Pacino, the rest of the cast can handle the dialogue without problems, but they don't have any passion for the words they are saying. Jeremy Irons as Antonio spends a lot of time looking off camera as if he's trying to locate the agent who landed him in this fiasco. Joseph Fiennes's Bassanio and Lynn Collins's Portia have no chemistry and their time together is so lacking any connection that it often feels like a split-screen effect. Veteran British TV comedy actors John Sessions and Anton Rodgers show up in small roles as Salerio and The Duke, but they have nothing to do except to look aghast at the fumbling and bumbling around them.

Radford tries to negate the antisemitic elements of *The Merchant of Venice* with a new prologue explaining the historic intolerance toward the Jews in sixteenth-century Europe. There are also scenes of a Jewish man being thrown by bullies into a canal and pious Jews praying in a synagogue. This is well-meaning, but Radford goes further to *oomph* up the film with more scenes not found in the original play: a lamb has its throat slit; Bassanio contemplates eating a decapitated pigeon; bare-breasted whores allow filthy men to fondle their bodies; and Bassanio and Antonio kiss on the lips in a manner which goes beyond mere friendship. This is not an adaptation of Shakespeare—it is a desecration.

Mr. Arkadin
(1955, directed by Orson Welles)

ORSON WELLES is considered by many film critics and scholars to be the greatest American director of all time. Yet his canon as a director is relatively limited: he only completed thirteen films between 1941 and 1977 (this does not include a residue of unfinished work, not to mention at least one completed film that was never released and is still unavailable for public viewing).

Somewhere in the middle of his cinematic output was a weird and silly movie called *Mr. Arkadin*, also released in some countries as *Confidential Report*. Anyone who believes Welles only made great films will be in for a happy shock here because *Mr. Arkadin* is a terrible movie. But it is a brilliantly terrible movie—so full of outlandish and extravagant self-indulgence that it is difficult not to be entertained by it. Even when the film becomes incoherently ridiculous, *Mr. Arkadin* is a guilty pleasure, sort of like junk food for cineastes.

Welles plays the title role of a mysterious millionaire with dark secrets to hide. Unfortunately, his performance is among the most ludicrous of his career, enhanced by a blatantly false beard and nose and a comic Russian accent, which makes him sound a lot like the Boris Badenov character from the *Rocky & Bullwinkle* cartoon series. Welles also shot his scenes primarily in tight close-up, obviously to emphasize Arkadin's menace, but also to hide the fact he was dreadfully overweight. In the relatively few shots where he is filmed full body, Welles's excess weight is quite a sight to behold. (Sadly, this was the start of an endless fight with obesity that he would never be able to conquer.)

Mr. Arkadin focuses on the investigation into the origins of the title character's wealth. The report is compiled by an American smuggler and petty crook named Guy Van Stratten, who does too good of a job digging up the facts of Arkadin's past: a wide collection of con artists, ex-cons, and miscreants are interviewed by Van Stratten only to be bumped off after their information is relayed. Van Stratten realizes a bit too late that Arkadin is using his information to permanently erase the loose threads of his past by eliminating those who know the truth about him.

And from here, *Mr. Arkadin* runs into two serious problems. The first is the casting of Robert Arden as Van Stratten. Arden was a minor British actor at the time of the film's production and he was genuinely shocked that Welles wanted him for the film. (Arden reportedly thought that Welles' phone inquiry offering him the role was a crank call.) Whether it was the inadequacy of the script or the actor's incompetence, Arden came across as thoroughly obnoxious and abrasive. Welles clearly did not see what other directors did, for Arden never played a starring role again.

Compounding this matter was Welles's curious decision to cast his wife, Italian countess and sometime-actress Paola Mori, in the key role as Arkadin's daughter. The film centers around Arkadin's obsession with keeping his daughter from learning the truth about his past. Mori turned out to be a terrible leading lady and Welles brought in British star Billie Whitelaw to dub her lines. But Mori's sultry Italian glamour was not matched by Whitelaw's posh Britspeak and the character wound up being wildly out of place and unfocused. As with Arden, this was her only starring role.

But being an Orson Welles production, the movie is not without its diversions. Welles managed to pack the film with a wealth of over-the-top cameos by some fine performers, including Michael Redgrave (as an effeminate antique dealer), Mischa Auer (as the creepy flea circus operator—Welles supposedly dubbed his lines), Patricia Medina (wife of Welles's one-time collaborator Joseph Cotten) as a dim moll, Katina Paxinou as the aged head of a former white slavery ring, and Akim Tamiroff as a dying crook; Tamiroff's wife, Tamara Shayne, has a bit part as a frantic landlady. The hammy excesses of these star turns coupled with Welles's trademark off-kilter camerawork keeps the viewer's attention long after the film's logic has evaporated.

Adding to the confusion was the absence of a definitive version of *Mr. Arkadin*. Instead, there are four different English-language versions and two different Spanish-language versions circulating about. But no matter which version you pick, *Mr. Arkadin* will not disappoint.

Mr. Freedom
(1969, directed by William Klein)

I AM SOMEWHAT EMBARRASSED to admit that I fell asleep when I first tried to watch William Klein's 1969 satire *Mr. Freedom*. This go-round in dreamland was, in retrospect, a bit surprising because I came to the film expecting a fast-paced, loud, chaotic assault on the funny bone.

Mr. Freedom opens in an American inner city during a riot. A cigar-smoking, beer-guzzling sheriff returns to his police station and pulls back a giant American flag covering a wall. Behind the flag is a closet containing the uniform of the superhero Mr. Freedom. This red, white, and blue get-up actually looks like a hodgepodge of football, baseball, and hockey uniforms.

Mr. Freedom, with guns blazing, goes into the night and bursts into the apartment of an African-American family. After shooting off some bullets, he breaks into his theme chant: "F-R-Double E-D-D-O-M!" Yeah, he spelled "freedom" wrong. It is not particularly funny the first time and it gets less amusing with the many reprises throughout the film.

Mr. Freedom is then summoned via a Dick Tracy-style wristwatch-TV to Freedom, Inc. headquarters by Dr. Freedom (played by British actor Donald Pleasence sporting a perfect American accent). Freedom, Inc. is housed in the same complex as imperialist conglomerates, including the United Fruit Company and Standard Oil. Dr. Freedom appears via flickering TV monitors to assign Mr. Freedom a trans-Atlantic mission: go to France to stop a Communist takeover. The previous Freedom, Inc. leader there, Capitaine Formidable (Yves Montand in an unbilled gag appearance) was murdered, so Mr. Freedom needs to save the French from the Reds.

In France, Mr. Freedom travels about Paris wearing a red shirt, white cowboy hat, and blue suit. He connects with Marie-Madeline, the widow of

Capitaine Formidable (Delphine Seyrig in a Little Orphan Annie wig and a drum majorette bodysuit). She, in turn, connects him with the local pro-Freedom, Inc. operatives (including singer Serge Gainsbourg, who never gets to sing despite hovering around a piano for most of his scenes).

During his Parisian journey, Mr. Freedom stops by the U.S. Embassy (which looks like a supermarket-department store) and he encounters various foes: Super French Man (a large human-shaped balloon), the Marxist gang leader Moujik Man (Philippe Noiret in a red balloon suit), Red China Man (a large dragon balloon with smoking nostrils), and the mother-son team of Mary and Jesus (yes, *them*).

Eventually, Mr. Freedom discovers the French don't want to be saved and abhor the American style of democracy. He decides the only thing that can save the French is destruction—so he sets off a nuclear device that wrecks France. He, of course, destroys himself in the process.

Writer/director Klein was an American expatriate who enjoyed a career in France as a fashion photographer and occasional documentary filmmaker and he obviously had a lot of anger against American society circa 1969. In some moments, he knows how to channel that anger (the embassy-hypermarket is a brilliant sight gag). And some bits of dialogue are very funny (especially when an exasperated Jesus cuts off his mother by insisting: "Mom, please!").

But on the whole, Klein is clueless when it comes to building comedy sequences. Most of his big sequences, such as Mr. Freedom's two pep rallies with his French supporters or the encounters with Moujik Man and Red China Man, are shapeless and pointless. And having Mr. Freedom rant about "niggers" and the need for white unity only further isolates the audience from the main character.

Needless to say, *Mr. Freedom 2* never came about. *Merci beaucoup!*

Moment by Moment
(1978, directed by Jane Wagner)

ONE OF THE MOST DRAMATIC comebacks in movie history took place in 1994 with John Travolta's performance in *Pulp Fiction*. Travolta had been considered a washed-up icon of the late 1970s, yet his hipster star-turn as the funky gangster offered an extraordinary second chance at A-list stardom.

But why was Travolta in need of a comeback? The answer can be traced back to *Moment by Moment*, a 1978 romantic drama that nearly knocked out his career following the one-two punch of *Saturday Night Fever* and *Grease*.

Moment by Moment was a peculiar vehicle for Travolta. The film was rooted in the collaborative force of Lily Tomlin and Jane Wagner. Wagner was responsible for writing most of Tomlin's classic comedy material and she was (and still is) her life partner. But rather than make a comedy, the women envisioned a weepy melodrama closer in spirit to the old Douglas Sirk soapers. Wagner wrote the screenplay and directed the film (her first time behind the camera) while Tomlin took on the role of Trish, a rich Beverly Hills divorcee who becomes infatuated with a sensitive young hustler.

Moment by Moment is pretty much a two-person movie, with Tomlin's rich Trish being pursued by Travolta's gabby hustler. That character's name is Strip, which is awkward because Tomlin often calls out to him: "Oh, Strip! Strip!" And yes, it gets embarrassing very quickly.

The characters meet at Schwab's Pharmacy when Trish is unable to renew a prescription for sleeping pills. Strip tracks her back to her palatial beach house, where he gives her a vial of "reds" to help her get a good night's snooze. Strip doesn't really go away—he keeps coming back to make stupid small talk, mostly regarding the mishaps of his jailed pal, Greg. Trish, who would've called the cops had she been a real person, indulges the handsome but verbose Strip with lunch and attention and she even shows a rare charitable side by offering to finance the repairs on Greg's dilapidated automobile, which doubles as Strip's temporary residence.

Needless to say, things get hot and heavy one rainy night when Trish takes Strip inside and makes him take off his wet clothing. She lays him down on a daybed, then lies down next to him, giving him a hand job. The expression on Travolta's face while his ding-a-ling gets a workout (his bovine eyes blinking with initial incomprehension) is among the most unintentionally hilarious moments captured on screen.

For the remainder of the film, Trish and Strip talk, make love, talk some more, make love again, fight, separate, and then reunite. Tomlin does a terrible imitation of a heterosexual woman rediscovering her sex drive via a young stud while Travolta just lies there like a slab of uncooked beef. You could find more eroticism in a stop-motion animated film using mannequins than in watching these two real people bang each other.

In the late 1990s, Travolta confided in an interview with Cranky-Critic.com about the near-fatal effects of *Moment by Moment* on his psyche and self-confidence:

> "I think I learned 20 years ago when I did *Saturday Night Fever* and *Grease* and was touted the biggest star in the world," Travolta recalled. "Then I did a movie called *Moment by Moment* and you'd have thought I'd sunk the Titanic. I was so mistreated as a result of that film that I can never again take any of it seriously. So I guess I learned that you've got to be tough and expect the worst, but nothing could be worse than that."

Mother Riley Meets the Vampire
(1952, directed by John Gilling)

MOTHER RILEY MEETS THE VAMPIRE marked a double-nadir for two icons of the silver screen: Bela Lugosi, the ultimate movie horror villain, and Arthur Lucan, who enjoyed a long and popular career in British films by putting on women's clothing and playing Old Mother Riley, a boisterous Irish washerwoman.

Mother Riley Meets the Vampire casts Lugosi as Von Housen, a mad scientist who wants to take over the world with an army of giant robots that run on uranium. To secure that power source, he kidnaps the daughter of an Italian scientist who has a map of a recently discovered South American uranium mine. Von Housen, by the way, sleeps in a coffin and wears a Dracula-worthy wardrobe. Although he fancies himself a vampire, everyone knows he is not.

Fate (actually, the Royal Mail) deals Von Housen's plans a blow when the delivery of a robot prototype is delivered to Old Mother Riley instead. Von Housen gets the washerwoman's package instead: a collection of bedpans and bottles left in an inheritance by a late uncle. Using telepathic skills, Von Housen activates the robot and has it kidnap Mother Riley. The washerwoman is surprised to find herself delivered to Von Housen's mansion, where the scientist employs her as a cleaning woman. He also considers her to be a juicy source of blood and feeds her a meat-heavy diet (steak for breakfast, liver for lunch, and beef for dinner) to make sure her type-O blood supply is high in iron. Mother Riley reacts to this strange diet by rolling her eyes and trying not to vomit.

Beyond this, Mother Riley discovers the abducted Italian girl (remember her?) with the help of a young maid (Dora Bryan). The police are called in and there is much mayhem with Mother Riley wrestling one of

Von Housen's robots before pursuing the scientist in a wild chase. Needless to say, Von Housen does not take over the world.

Mother Riley Meets the Vampire is one of the most aggressively unfunny comedies to come out of the U.K. Even Lugosi, who could easily parody his Dracula image, is barely functioning here. He seems more like a zombie than a vampire, dropping his lines so carelessly that it seems he was spitting them out so as not to be burdened with a rancid aftertaste.

As for Lucan, forget it. He fought a long and unsuccessful fight with alcoholism and his ragged appearance and dull comic timing show the ravages of the disease. He is unable to find anything new or interesting to do with his character, so he repeats the same level of noisy knockabout from his previous movies. Thus, there are endless yelling matches with angry rent collectors, endless skewering of the English language, endless gasps at being threatened by various miscreants, endless pratfalls in slapstick violence— yes, the film truly feels endless!

Although Lucan was very popular in Britain, the film bombed upon its initial release. No American distributor would touch it, so plans were considered to delete the scenes with Lucan and incorporate Lugosi's scenes into a new American production. However, nothing came of that.

The film was unseen stateside until a company called Blue Chip Productions obtained it in 1963 (seven years after Lugosi's death). The title was changed to *Carry On Vampire*, which was meant to cash in on the *Carry On* comedy films from Britain. When the *Carry On* producers sent a cease-and-desist notice, the film was then retitled *My Son, the Vampire* and a new introduction was shot featuring comedian Allan Sherman. Over the years, the film popped up with the titles *Vampire Over London*, *The Vampire and the Robot*, and even *Dracula's Desire*.

Mommie Dearest
(1981, directed by Frank Perry)

FEW SUBJECTS ARE AS GRIM and disturbing as child abuse. Yet one of the reigning works of unintentional comedy is centered on the abusive relationship between a parent and a child.

In 1978, Christina Crawford published the tell-all autobiography *Mommie Dearest*. The maternal figure in the title was Hollywood legend Joan Crawford, who adopted Christina and three other children during the 1940s. In *Mommie Dearest*, Christina offered a harsh and harrowing account of her life, which included sensational accusations of physical and emotional abuse dished out by Joan Crawford, who had died from cancer one year before the book was published.

Christina eagerly sold the film rights to *Mommie Dearest* to Paramount Pictures and the project took on the trappings of a prestige project when Oscar-winning actress Faye Dunaway was signed to play Joan Crawford. But much to everyone's shock, the film version of *Mommie Dearest* transformed Christina's dark story into a wild, uninhibited camp fest that convulsed audiences with unexpected gales of laughter.

How did this happen? For the most part, the blame was centered solely on Dunaway's performance as Crawford. Rather than try to plumb the soul of her character and attempt to locate whatever shreds of humanity remained in the supposedly monstrous movie star-mother, Dunaway instead appeared to be imitating Carol Burnett's famous imitation of Crawford—complete with Groucho Marx-worthy eyebrows and excessive shoulder pads. Dunaway also embraced the Carol Burnett exaggeration of Crawford's highly stylized physical mannerisms and line readings—all very amusing for a ten-minute parody skit on a comedy show, but out of place in a feature-length film with no comedic aspirations.

The real challenge for Dunaway was to show Crawford's periods of manic behavior and the reckless manner in which she terrorized her adopted daughter. In her approach to the role, Dunaway channeled Crawford's larger-than-life screen persona to create a larger-than-life off-screen monster. Dunaway pops her eyes, knits her eyebrows, bares her teeth with wolverine fury, and convulses her body into a riot of tremors. As this takes place, she spits out her dialogue at high-decibel roars that seem to place emphasis on nearly every word.

Of course, the film became infamous for the scene where the fastidious Crawford discovers one of Christina's dresses hanging in a closet on a wire hanger. Crawford, angry that the child would hang her expensive dress on a flimsy hanger, erupts in a volcanic rage. "NO… WIRE… HANGERS… EVER!" roared Dunaway's Crawford, turning the most benign of domestic infractions into a denunciation of operatic proportions.

Further complicating matters was Dunaway's delivery of salty lines that were meant to show the steely side of Crawford's personality. However, the actress played the dialogue for cheap laughs, throwing out lines like "Tear down that BITCH of a bearing wall and put a window where it OUGHT to be" and "Don't fuck with me, fellas—this ain't my first time at the rodeo" with an over-the-top bravado that echoed the aforementioned Carol Burnett spoofing of the classic Crawford melodramas.

Variety, in its review of *Mommie Dearest*, picked up on this weird and wild interpretation of Crawford's book. "This is Faye Dunaway as Joan Crawford and the results are, well, screen history," the trade magazine commented in its review. "Dunaway does not chew scenery. Dunaway starts neatly at each corner of the set in every scene and swallows it whole, costars and all."

But no one quite expected what happened next. While promoted as a straightforward biopic with serious undertones—the studio carefully planted buzz that Dunaway would be in line for a Best Actress Oscar—*Mommie Dearest* began to gain an audience that saw the film very differently. Some screenings took on the trappings of *Rocky Horror Picture Show*-style audience participation with gay male patrons dressed up as the extravagant Joan Crawford and chasing other patrons pretending to be Christina with wire hangers and cans of Ajax cleaner.

Paramount Pictures decided to cash in on this unexpected phenomenon by switching its marketing approach one month into the film's release. New advertisements included the text "No wire hangers… ever!" and identified Crawford as "the biggest mother of them all." This marketing switch was done without informing the film's producer, Frank Yablans, who promptly sued Paramount for $5 million and berated the new advertisements by claiming they were "obscene, vulgar, offensive, salacious, and embodied a racial slur of the poorest taste."

Mommie Dearest was a box office hit, but its reputation was permanently ruined by the absurdity of its presentation. The film won five Razzie Awards, including Worst Picture and Worst Actress, and it would later win the Worst Picture of the Decade Razzie at the tail end of the 1980s. Dunaway's reputation as a serious actress also suffered as quality roles became increasingly scarce after the *Mommie Dearest* dust settled. To this date, the actress refuses to answer any interview questions regarding the film.

Still, there was an immortality of sorts. *Mommie Dearest* has become a cult classic, especially among gay audiences that laugh at Dunaway's drag queen approach to her role. Dunaway's performance ranked her #41 on the American Film Institute's list of 100 Heroes & Villains, while "No wire hangers, ever!" came in #72 on the institute's list of 100 Movie Quotes—two achievements that bring smiles when they should bring chills.

Mourning Becomes Electra
(1947, directed by Dudley Nichols)

EUGENE O'NEILL'S THEATRICAL adaptation of Aeschylus's *Oresteia* trilogy set in a nineteenth-century New England environment created a six-hour trilogy titled *Mourning Becomes Electra*. The film version of this theatrical event boiled the O'Neill text down to a three-hour running time, but it remained uncommonly long for a non-epic motion picture.

The crux of the story remained intact: the Mannon family is in turmoil when the patriarch, Brigadier General Ezra Mannon, returns home in poor health from the Civil War. His wife, Christine, who always loathed him, has been carrying on an affair with the dashing sea captain Adam Brant. Their daughter, Lavinia, whose devotion to her father borders on incestuous, discovers her mother's infidelity and is fueled by twin passions: her long-simmering hatred of her mother and her own unrequited love for the handsome sea captain. Then there is Orin Mannon, the son of Ezra and Christine, who comes home with his own war injuries. When Ezra dies suddenly, Lavinia and Orin conspire to enact revenge against their mother by murdering her lover. Rather than bring closure, this only creates more bloody complications.

Clearly there is a great story in here. But sadly, *Mourning Becomes Electra* went haywire thanks in large part to its casting.

The central character of Lavinia was played by Rosalind Russell, who plumbs the character's turmoil and comes up with sawdust melodrama acting: intense glaring, fists clutching her heart, screaming in lieu of speaking, and a perpetual sneer. At forty years old, she was also two decades too old for the role (she actually looks much older on screen). Her scenes with Katina Paxinou, who plays her mother, are extremely awkward since Paxinou was seven years her senior in real life and the women seemed more like sisters than mother and child.

Paxinou's presence is equally problematic. The only possible reason the Greek actress was cast here was because the role of Christine was originally played on Broadway by the great Russian star Alla Nazimova and it was assumed someone with a heavy accent had to fill the role. Paxinou was no slouch in the overacting department, but here she is so stiff that it appears rigor mortis is taking over. The searing fury of O'Neill's dialogue is lost in her thick, icy line readings. Rather than inspire scalding emotions by those around her, she seems to encourage overacting by the rest of the cast, who may have felt a void in her presence.

And the overacting here is not in short supply. The normally reliable Raymond Massey has the funniest death scene imaginable as Ezra Mannon—he often seems unable to keep a straight face in this film. English actor Michael Redgrave was inexplicably imported to play Orin Mannon. His attempts at a New England accent keep failing and his broad portrayal of the sensitive son makes him seem like a big sissy. Another English actor, Leo Genn, keeps his real life accent to play Adam Brant, but his manners are so polite and dignified that it is impossible to imagine him as a briny nineteenth-century sea captain. Kirk Douglas shows up as Lavinia's suitor, but his sunny and eager-to-please, all-American demeanor seems way out of place in this gloomy tragedy—you feel as if he wandered over from the set of *Our Town* by accident.

RKO initially released *Mourning Becomes Electra* as a road show attraction and the result was a box office catastrophe. Even Oscar nominations for Redgrave and Russell failed to quell the disaster. The studio quickly cut the film to 105 minutes, which made a thorough mess of the narrative. Those who did bother to show up to view it were confused by what they were watching. A two-hour version was later offered, but it made no difference. For the British release, the film played at 159 minutes.

Despite the various versions, *Mourning Becomes Electra* lost $3 million for the studio—which, for RKO, was something worth mourning.

Move
(1970, directed by Stuart Rosenberg)

THIS FILM HAS ALL BUT DISAPPEARED from cinematic culture, which is odd considering its pedigree. A 20th Century Fox release, it was directed by Stuart Rosenberg (best known for helming *Cool Hand Luke*) and stars Elliott Gould at the peak of his popularity in the early 1970s.

Gould plays Hiram Jaffe, a would-be Manhattan playwright who cannot get a crumb of interest from any theatrical producer. He supplements his income by writing pornographic fiction and walking the dogs of his neighborhood's wealthier residents. It would seem that he is only able to maintain a one-room apartment in New York's Upper West Side because his wife Dolly (Paula Prentiss) has a steady job as a psychiatrist's receptionist. An oversized St. Bernard named Murphy serves as Jaffe's companion when he faces his daily frustrations—most egregiously from a sourpuss mounted patrolman in Central Park who is constantly ticketing Hiram for some inane infraction.

For no clear reason—after all, Hiram is barely making money and Dolly does not seem to have any additional source of income—the couple is able to secure a larger apartment elsewhere in their neighborhood. They have their lives packed up in moving crates and are eager to relocate. However, the moving man they've hired proves to be elusive and repeated telephone calls to get him to offer the services he's been paid to perform are met with delays, excuses, and evasions.

To escape from the tedium of his existence, Hiram finds himself escaping into weird fantasies where he gets to strip off his clothing. Whether the sight of Gould's hairy nakedness is supposed to be sexy or funny is not clear, but he usually winds up yelling and performing weird tasks, such as painting his new apartment while nude. This escape from reality eventually brings him in contact with a hot blonde with an open mind and open legs (Geneviève Waïte, a South African model-singer who would later marry John Phillips of The Mamas & The Papas).

Move can be described as an unholy mix of Neil Simon and Federico Fellini, although I fear that would make it seem much more interesting than it is. The Felliniesque touches begin in the opening credits, which find Gould walking down Manhattan's streets while the rest of the pedestrian traffic walks backward. Gould then gets his feet stuck in asphalt while a steamroller drives over him, creating a cartoonish flattened image.

More Fellini-inspired nonsense involves Hiram's overbaked sexual fantasies and *Move* took full advantage of the early 1970s' free-wheeling spirit by pushing its R-rating with flashes of bare breasts and shots of Gould's naked backside. But the effect is puerile and sophomoric and what little shock exists quickly evaporates as the film progresses.

As for the Neil Simon element, *Move* is the type of film where the characters speak in wisecracks and sarcasm instead of normal conversation. For example, an exasperated Hiram bemoans his dog-walking duties by proclaiming he was a "grown man coaxing dogs to move their bowels!" When Dolly starts showing evidence of wanting a family, Hiram snaps, "Gee, Dolly, what's this insane passion to bring babies into the world?" And those are the film's funnier lines!

Move was the final film produced by the legendary Pandro S. Berman, who was responsible for some of the greatest RKO and MGM films from Hollywood's golden age. What a way to end a career!

Mystic River
(2003, directed by Clint Eastwood)

WHILE BELOVED AS A LEGEND on both sides of the camera, Clint Eastwood has created a surprisingly large number of films that run the gamut from mediocre to atrocious. (Lest we forget: *Firefox*; *The Rookie*; *White Hunter, Black Heart*; *Midnight in the Garden of Good and Evil*; *Space Cowboys*; *Blood Work*; *Gran Torino*; *Invictus*; and *Hereafter*.) And yes, this film adaptation of Dennis Lehane's thriller picked up some prestigious awards. But so what? Forget its pedigree and its trophies—this production is so incredibly off-kilter that it demands attention for its sheer awfulness.

The film opens in the 1970s in a less-desirable section of Boston. Three boys—Jimmy (the wise guy with red hair), Sean (the good kid), and Dave (the big doofus)—are playing in the street when a car pulls up and two men posing as cops begin harassing the kids. Dave is taken away in the car and the men hold him in pedophiliac captivity for four days. Dave escapes, but the emotional damage is severe—so severe that he grows up to be Tim Robbins pretending to be a dumb, creepy, chronically unemployed guy. Dave behaves a lot like Lon Chaney, Jr.'s Lennie from *Of Mice and Men* and his shallowness is matched by his even dumber wife (Marcia Gay Harden, who seems to be channeling Jean Stapleton's Edith Bunker).

Sean grows up to be a cop, played by Kevin Bacon. Sean has an annoying wife who left him while she was pregnant. She constantly calls him, but refuses to say a word. Sadly, no one bothered to throw in one of those "Can you hear me now?" taglines from the telephone commercials (although *Mystic River* has some fine cameo appearances by Jack Daniel's, Jell-O pudding, and Sprite—and, at one point, a can of Sprite actually becomes the heart of a crucial scene).

The third kid, Jimmy, grows up without his red hair (it gets coal-black with a touch of gray). He now bears a striking resemblance to Sean Penn. This Jimmy did a two-year jail stint rather than snitch on his hoodlum pals. He now runs a convenience store, but he still has his fingers on the pulse of the underworld and chums with a miscreant sibling duo named (what else?) the Savage Brothers. He has a wife (played by Laura Linney) who doesn't do anything until the final ten minutes of the film when she abruptly lets loose with a Lady Macbeth-worthy soliloquy which seems to have been inserted from another story.

Oh, there is also Laurence Fishburne as Sean's partner on the police force. He's the token black comedy relief here: he doesn't have a wife or even a girlfriend and his character is named Whitey.

Okay, so what's the point? Well, Jimmy's nineteen-year-old daughter is murdered in her car in a park (or, in the film's approximation of the Boston accent, *in hah cah in da pahk*). The same night, Dave comes home with blood on his clothing, a knife gash across his belly, and a banged up hand. Dave's wife thinks he killed Jimmy's daughter. Soon, the cops are starting to suspect Dave. And then Jimmy suspects Dave, too.

But another possible killer emerges: the career criminal whose plea deal put Jimmy in jail years ago. It seems the bullet from the crime scene matched a bullet in a 1984 liquor store hold-up. And as luck would have it, this guy's son was going to run off to Las Vegas with Jimmy's daughter for a quickie wedding the day after she was killed.

Mystic River has the foundations for both a tragedy and a mystery, but instead, the film is directed like a comedy. Specifically, a Mack Sennett silent comedy with a surplus of exaggerated, overstated, Acting 101 performances. But the strange thing is that all of the actors seem to be emoting while running an inner rehearsal on how to thank the Academy—how else can one explain so much grand exposition on so little material?

Some fun can be found in trying to figure out who gives the worst performance. Is it Sean Penn, complete with gnashing teeth and tightly flexed biceps, imitating Frank Gorshin's celebrated imitation of Kirk Douglas? Or is it Laurence Fishburne, who does such a killer Lou Rawls-style, self-assured turn that he literally glides through his scenes? Or is it Marcia Gay Harden, whose gaping mouth and wide-eye stare recall a fish on ice? Or Laura Linney, who fills her mouth with so many flattened vowels that chalk on a blackboard would be more soothing to the ears?

Or perhaps it is the joker in the pack: the eternal ham Eli Wallach, who makes a surprise cameo as the liquor store owner? Wallach huffs and puffs so much in his brief scene that you wish he could blow the film down.

But the real bad performer is behind the camera: Clint Eastwood, who infects the film with the same inertia and fumbling he's brought to many of the films he's directed. Scenes are badly blocked, the lighting is either a rip-off of silent German expressionist art movies or is badly illuminated to the point that all color is drained, key players are miscast (Kevin Bacon in particular, who barely registers on-screen here), and the music is wildly inappropriate (scored by Eastwood himself, borrowing heavily from Carl Orff's excessive compositions). And talk about too much of a bad thing: the 137-minute film runs a good twenty minutes too long, while the final dozen minutes make no sense whatsoever.

The best thing about *Mystic River* is the river. Like its Mississippi cousin, it just keeps rolling along.

The Negro Soldier
(1944, directed by Stuart Heisler)

DURING WORLD WAR II, the American military effort was seriously disfigured due to the nation's cruel and hostile policies regarding racial segregation. Despite wartime media censorship designed to squash inklings of a fragmented home front, it was no secret that African-American civil rights leaders and the black military personnel angrily pressed for fair treatment and a greater level of participation in the actual frontline battles.

The sensitivity of the matter resulted in a decision by the War Department (the forerunner of today's Department of Defense) to create a propagandistic documentary designed to boost the perceived value of the African-American contribution to the wartime effort. The resulting film, however, turned out to be a shocking work of intellectual dishonesty: *The Negro Soldier*, a 1944 production that, pardon the pun, whitewashed not only the state of race relations during that era, but also shamelessly rewrote American history to create a utopian environment where racism never existed.

From the beginning, *The Negro Soldier* created hackles for all involved. Frank Capra, who was the head of the War Department's film endeavors (his *Why We Fight* series helped ready the nation for the conflict), was reluctant to pursue this project despite a direct order from General George C. Marshall to create a movie on the subject. Instead, Capra shucked the directing responsibility to Stuart Heisler.

The Negro Soldier opens in an all-black church. After the choir sings a comforting hymn, a minister begins a sermon paying tribute to the congregation members who are currently in service. The minister then begins reading from Hitler's *Mein Kampf* to emphasize the racist philosophies that drive Nazism (Hitler referred to blacks as "half-apes"). The film then goes back to the American Revolution to show African-American contributions to the nation's many military struggles. Beginning with Crispus Attucks at the Boston Massacre, the film highlights several black heroes of the revolution and the later War of 1812.

Then the film hopscotches to the Civil War, which is presented in fifteen seconds. Then it focuses on the taming of the Wild West. And then… uh, aren't we forgetting something in this history lesson? Yes, *The Negro Soldier* blithely fails to mention slavery. As the film spins American history, blacks and whites lived in the pre-Civil War years as equals in an integrated society. We see dramatic scenes of black men and white men in early nineteenth-century costumes working together as equals on industrial and agricultural projects. The film gives no reason for why the Civil War happened and it never mentions the Emancipation Proclamation or the Thirteenth Amendment to the Constitution. It also never mentions Jim Crow or Plessy v. Ferguson.

The military history lesson fails to mention the celebrated Buffalo Soldiers, but it does provide citations of African-American soldiers who performed above and beyond the call of duty in the Spanish-American War and World War I. At no time in the film is there mention that black soldiers served in racially segregated units.

The film then traces contemporary African-American achievement by showing a number of prominent people from various professions. None of these people are identified by name, although it is easy enough to identify the surgeon Dr. Charles Drew and the contralto Marian Anderson. There is also a bootlegged clip (complete with the original narration) from Leni Riefenstahl's *Olympia* that shows the victories of Jesse Owens at the 1936 Berlin Olympics.

The film then abruptly switches to the present-day army. From here, it becomes even more ridiculous. The military induction and processing system is presented as a racially integrated endeavor with blacks and whites freely intermingling. From there, the black soldiers are abruptly shown at a blacks-only training base. There is also a blacks-only USO canteen sequence. Where did the white people go? Who knows—nobody mentions their absence.

The Negro Soldier avoids any mention of black combat efforts on the front lines, which is understandable since, at the time when the film was shot (1942 and 1943), blacks were kept out of frontline combat. The fabled Tuskegee Airmen are shown in training, but the film reminds us they were only in training and had yet to go into battle.

The film occasionally cuts back to the church setting, where at one point, a woman from the congregation rises to read a letter from her son in the army. The letter details how the young man is being fast-tracked for officer's training—but, of course, the film never mentions that officer opportunities for African-Americans were relatively scarce in the World War II military.

The Negro Soldier was first shown to the segregated black troops in January 1944. The reaction was, at best, peculiar; according to *Time* magazine, the soldiers watched the fractured history lesson in shocked silence, but afterward requested that the film be shown to white audiences.

But few people of any race saw the film. The various Hollywood studios that volunteered to release War Department productions to theaters refused to touch it, thus requiring the War Department to play distributor and release the movie itself. The theatrical release, however, was severely limited to approximately 1,800 theaters—there were about 13,000 cinemas in the United States at the time.

Reviews of *The Negro Soldier* were cautious; there was praise for the concept, but not the execution. The *New York Times* diplomatically stated, "It is to be noted that it very discreetly avoids the more realistic race problems which are generally recognized today. It definitely sugar coats an issue that is broader than the Negro's part in the war. For this reason, it is questionable whether the purpose which it is intended now to serve publicly may not be defeated by the film's own limitations and lacks."

Time magazine was even more blunt: "As anyone can see who knows or cares anything about the seriousness of the subject, the makers of the film have not included any of the dynamite implicit in a truly forthright treatment of the subject. There is no mention of segregation, of friction between Negro soldiers and white soldiers and civilians."

Paul McCartney Really Is Dead: The Last Testament of George Harrison?
(2010, directed by Joel Gilbert)

A GREAT DEAL OF THE MAGIC of motion pictures comes from the audience's ability to suspend practical thought and accept the most outlandish concepts imaginable. But this basic tenet of film appreciation is stretched far beyond the fraying point with Joel Gilbert's utterly ridiculous pseudo-documentary *Paul McCartney Really Is Dead: The Last Testament of George Harrison?*, which is rooted in the insistence that George Harrison left behind audio recordings that confirmed the late 1960s urban legend of Paul McCartney's automobile accident death and secret replacement by a ringer.

Highway 61 Entertainment, the company behind this film, insists that in 2005, it received a parcel from London that contained a microcassette recorder and two tapes narrated by someone who supposedly sounded like Harrison. The parcel had no return address and there was no explanation why that particular company—as opposed to a serious news organization—was chosen to receive the material.

This film, which is narrated by someone that sounds absolutely nothing like Harrison, details the circumstances of McCartney's alleged demise (he was supposedly decapitated in a car crash) and how the cover-up took root (MI5, the UK equivalent of the CIA, determined that news of McCartney's death would cause mass suicides, so a look-alike replacement was recruited). The replacement, a Canadian named William Campbell, undergoes plastic surgery to alter his appearance to resemble McCartney's, but the other Beatles resent this charade and refer to their new band member as "Faul" (short for "False Paul"); they also sprinkle clues in their songs and album cover designs about the presence of the impostor.

In the course of its ninety-five minutes, this film runs through an inventory of every well-worn conspiracy allegation as proof of the "Paul is dead" scenario. Yes, all the oddball album covers, pun-filled lyrics, backward-played music, and curiously posed photographs are trotted out and presented as the honest-to-goodness truth. There are also a few new claims, such as tying the murder of John Lennon to an MI5 plot to keep the "Faul" story under wraps. The film also insists that Heather Mills (McCartney's second wife) was a hitchhiking passenger in the car that McCartney drove to his death. Never mind that she was born two years *after* the crash supposedly occurred!

Beatles fans might have some fun with the wealth of vintage news footage and photographs that are gathered here. However, none of the Fab Four's songs were licensed, so the viewer is unable to actually hear the alleged clues dropped in the song lyrics. And those with only a passing knowledge of Beatles trivia will easily recognize some obvious historical errors (the film claims that clues about "Faul" first appeared on the *Rubber Soul* album, which was released *before* McCartney's alleged death).

Conspiracy theorists could easily get indigestion gobbling up the film's servings. But anyone with limited patience for cinematic stupidity can stop this mess at any point and drive the Magical Mystery Tour bus through the film's holes of logic. Mother Mary really did say it best: let it be.

Plan 9 from Outer Space
(1959, directed by Edward D. Wood, Jr.)

When it comes to naming the best film ever made, a lively and spirited debate will inevitably occur. There will be fanboys insistent on *Star Wars*, cinephiles advocating *Citizen Kane*, champions of old Hollywood insisting on *Gone with the Wind* or *Casablanca*, and the cult worshippers pushing anything from Hitchcock, Kurosawa, or John Waters.

But when it comes to naming the worst film ever made, there is an almost unanimous candidate that gets pegged for that sorry title: Edward D. Wood, Jr.'s *Plan 9 from Outer Space*.

The notion of *Plan 9 from Outer Space* as the worst of the worst can be credited (or blamed) on the Medved Brothers, Harry and Michael (yes, *that* Michael Medved, before he became a right-wing kook). Their 1980 book *The Golden Turkey Awards* parodied the Oscars by offering awards for the least successful achievements in movie history. While the "winners" were fairly subjective (Richard Burton and Raquel Welch were named Worst Actor and Worst Actress of All Time), the choice of *Plan 9 from Outer Space* as the worst film ever seemed to click with the general public. (Wood never knew of these unlikely accolades, having died of a heart attack a year before *The Golden Turkey Awards* was published.)

But is *Plan 9 from Outer Space* deserving of its reputation? I don't think so and there are four clear reasons why.

First, *Plan 9 from Outer Space* is clearly a very entertaining movie, if only for the wrong reasons, and one can easily come away from the film with a hearty (if slightly guilty) smile at its blatantly cheapjack production, purple prose, shoddy special effects, and overcooked acting. But can a film that makes you feel good really be the worst of cinema?

Second, the incompetence of Wood's screenplay and direction is actually a case of enthusiasm running ahead of talent. Although he clearly could not funnel his grand ideas into a puny budget, Wood was genuinely trying for something grander than Grade Z sci-fi. Indeed, his notion of "solaranite" as a substance that can set off an intergalactic firestorm to destroy the universe is a masterwork of cockamamie science. Compared to the other directors nominated by the Medveds as the worst of all time (William Beaudine, Herschell Gordon Lewis, and Phil Tucker), Wood is actually far more imaginative than his competition.

Third, if we are judging the worst movie of all time as a low-budget affair, there are countless other flicks that were incapable of disguising the poverty of their productions: the aforementioned *The Creeping Terror* and *Manos: The Hands of Fate* betray incompetent production values that make *Plan 9* look like *Avatar* in comparison.

Fourth, the notion of a "worst film of all time" is as elusive as a "best film of all time." Unless you've seen every single film that has been released, you cannot possibly make a statement of one film being superior to or inferior to all of the other flicks ever made.

Oddly, the beloved *Mystery Science Theater 3000* never included *Plan 9 from Outer Space* in the Satellite of Love's screening room. Considering which films were merciless roasted by that show, it says something about the value of *Plan 9*.

Of course, that's not to say that *Plan 9* isn't *one* of the greatest bad films of all time. But reserving space for it at the very bottom of the barrel is mighty unfair.

Reefer Madness
(1936, directed by Louis Gasnier)

REEFER MADNESS holds a weird distinction as being one of the most significant productions in the development of film appreciation. This is a fairly unusual fact considering there is relatively little of redeeming value to appreciate in this film.

First created in 1936 under the title *Tell Your Children*, the film was financed by a Christian group with the goal of educating parents on the dangers of juvenile marijuana usage. The film had a relatively scant release and was mostly ignored until 1938 when exploitation filmmaker Dwain Esper bought the rights to the film and changed the title to *Reefer Madness*. The title's slang reference to marijuana (which was taboo in the Hollywood studio system under the restrictive Production Code) helped to titillate audiences that ventured into the hazy world of "adults only" cinemas that existed on the fringe of the motion picture industry. The film would be recycled for years under a variety of titles, including *The Burning Question*, *Dope Addict*, *Doped Youth*, and (somewhat illogically) *Love Madness*.

Eventually, the film's theatrical potential was exhausted and it remained forgotten for decades. In 1971, Keith Stroup, founder of the marijuana legalization group National Organization for the Reform of Marijuana Laws (NORML), tracked down the film to the Library of Congress and purchased a print for $297. Stroup then engaged an up-and-coming distribution company called New Line Cinema to book *Reefer Madness* at college campuses and in the early days of the midnight movie circuit.

Young hipster audiences in the early 1970s fell in love with *Reefer Madness*. What was uncommon was that the film's popularity had nothing to do with cinematic excellence; instead, audiences viewed the film's ineptitude as a masterwork of unintentional comedy. The belated popularity of the film created the concept of the so-bad-it's-good flick, which, in turn, gave a new cult classic status to a wave of long-forgotten stinkers that were cheered for their sheer awfulness. *Reefer Madness* was the first film to enable appreciation of old-time cinematic turkeys.

In the film's convoluted plot, a pair of marijuana dealers—an unmarried couple that live together, but maintain separate beds—ply their trade on naïve teenagers. The teens (who, quite frankly, look too mature to be mistaken for minors) immediately get hooked after a puff or two on a joint. As a result of this newfound marijuana addiction, the film's characters devolve into exaggerated agents of violence and reckless behavior with an occasional timeout for a supersonic, reefer-fueled piano recital. Things eventually get out of hand with one guy going insane (we know he is damaged by his popped eyes and snarls) and a woman taking a suicidal plunge rather than going to jail.

Reefer Madness suffers from the vices of too many 1930s exploitation films: a dreary visual style, cheapjack production, and a sledgehammer level of subtlety in exploring its subject matter. But the film stands out for the actors' absurd reactions to taking a whiff of cannabis. Its exaggerated depiction of eye-rolling, manic, borderline-psychotic pot smokers is so bizarre that even the most conservative anti-drug warrior would have to laugh along with its sheer inanity.

Did anyone connected to the film know the real effects of marijuana? It is hard to say. A lot of the over-the-top acting in the film might be the fault of director Louis Gasnier, a veteran of the silent movies who never quite managed to adapt his style to the talkies. As a result, a great deal of *Reefer Madness* unfolds like a silent movie projected at the wrong speed: everything is too fast and too jerky for comfort.

Being a public domain film, *Reefer Madness* has been endlessly duped and colorized by anyone who can get hold of a print. It has even been adapted into a stage musical, where the camp elements were pressed even further.

Renaldo and Clara
(1978, directed by Bob Dylan)

SOMETHING WAS BLOWIN' in the wind back in 1978 and it wasn't a good movie! The one-time director Robert Zimmerman (aka Bob Dylan) put down his guitar, picked up a viewfinder, and brought forth something that could charitably be described as the single biggest waste of celluloid in the entire history of motion pictures.

Unlike classic baddies such as *Plan 9 From Outer Space* or *Manos: The Hands of Fate*, *Renaldo and Clara* does not have the so-bad-it's-good charm. You cannot laugh along, *MST3K*-style, at its clueless excesses. Instead, you are left numb, dumb, and completely baffled at the thorough incoherence and painful lethargy of this endeavor. If I could, to borrow a Cher lyric, turn back time—well, I would turn back the four hours (yes, *four hours*) of *Renaldo and Clara*'s running time that I put myself through.

Four hours of what? Even after watching it, I have no idea what the f--k the movie is supposed to be about. Bob Dylan plays Renaldo and his then-wife Sara plays Clara. Who these people are and what they are supposed to do is never defined. Three-hundred-pound Ronnie Hawkins plays Bob Dylan and Ronee Blakley (fresh off her Oscar-nominated performance in *Nashville*) plays Sara Dylan. Joan Baez is a character called the Woman in White—if only because she wears white in the movie. Baez's character and Sara are at odds over Renaldo's love, or maybe not.

Much of the footage was shot during Dylan's now-legendary Rolling Thunder tour, although the reasons for Dylan's eccentric on-stage appearance (wearing plastic masks or white paint on his face) is never explained.

In the course of the film, folk singer David Blue plays pinball alongside a swimming pool (huh?) while talking about New York's Greenwich Village in the late 1950s and 1960s. A group of street preachers hector indifferent New Yorkers about the alleged end of the world. A belly dancer entertains restaurant patrons by wiggling her solar plexus to "Hava Nagila," followed by a sleazy lounge singer performing "Willkommen" from the musical *Cabaret*, who is then followed on stage by Beat poet Allen Ginsberg. Then we cut back to David Blue at his pinball machine. Then we go to an Indian reservation. Then Ginsberg returns to read poetry.

It is not surprising that Steve Puchalski, the editor of *Shock Cinema*, described the film as being "edited together with a Weed Eater." Midway through the movie, the action switches into a concert benefit for Rubin "Hurricane" Carter, the boxer who was framed for murder in a controversial and long-running criminal case. Some scenes later, Harry Dean Stanton turns up as a convict escaping from prison. Joan Baez and Sara Dylan later turn up in a bordello dressed like prostitutes. Dylan (the real one, not Ronnie Hawkins) sings part of "House of the Rising Sun." Allen Ginsberg returns to recite his classic poem "Kaddish" while a woman in gypsy clothing massages his head. David Blue comes back later to play more pinball (perhaps he thought he was filming *Tommy*?). Ginsberg returns to dance (to what?). The film closes with a black woman, who is never identified and who played no part in the previous four hours, singing about "castles in the shifting sands."

Every now and then, Dylan sings something. Often the performances are magical (his cover of Hank Williams's "Kaw-Liga," plus "Tangled Up in Blue" and "Knockin' on Heaven's Door" are standouts), but more often than not, he is a sullen and shadowy presence. A variety of oddballs ranging from Sam Shepard (in his film debut) to Ramblin' Jack Elliott to Roger McGuinn pop up here and there.

(This summary fails to take into account the endless and pointless symbolism of such objects as flowers, horse-drawn carriages, rooms full of senior citizens, and Jack Kerouac's grave—all of which figure prominently throughout the film).

In an interview with *Playboy* timed to the film's release, Dylan blithely declared *Renaldo and Clara* to be a "very open movie." He also acknowledged the film (much of it financed by himself) ran far beyond its projected $600,000 budget—Dylan told the *Playboy* interviewer that his previous two tours existed to raise funds for this project.

Renaldo and Clara opened to overwhelmingly hostile and bewildered reviews, although a few critics (most notably David Sterritt of the *Christian Science Monitor*) were charitable in praising its disregard for the conservative aspects of linear storytelling. Audiences, though, stayed away in droves; after a scant eight-city release, Dylan recut the film to a two-hour version, then withdrew the film from circulation. The four-hour version turned up on YouTube in an unauthorized posting in 2011, but was quickly removed for copyright violation. To date, it remains hidden from view.

The Room
(2003, directed by Tommy Wiseau)

SCOTT FOUNDAS OF *VARIETY* was one of the very few critics to pay attention to *The Room* when it rolled into Hollywood in 2003. At the time, Foundas saw no future for the film. "Given audience reaction at screening attended, pic may be something of a first: A movie that prompts most of its viewers to ask for their money back—before even thirty minutes have passed," he wrote.

Little did Foundas imagine that this obscure indie production would become a cult movie phenomenon, albeit for reasons that were never anticipated by the individuals associated with its creation—especially its one-in-a-million director/producer/writer/star, Tommy Wiseau.

Wiseau is probably the closest thing that contemporary cinema has to a man of mystery. Even his date and place of birth are unclear. In interviews, Wiseau has claimed a 1968 birth in New Orleans, but in *The Room* (which was shot in 2002) he appears far beyond thirty-four years old, while his peculiar accented voice (which carries a distinctive Eastern European cadence) does not sound like it originated around Bourbon Street.

Wiseau's arrival in show business came in 2001 with an early version of *The Room* as a would-be theatrical play. Unable to get his work staged by a professional theater group, he then attempted to turn it into a novel. When publishers rejected the work, Wiseau raised $6 million to create a film version. How he raised this impressive sum is also somewhat mysterious, with Wiseau vaguely mentioning profits from the import of Korean-made leather jackets.

As a neophyte filmmaker, Wiseau ran up extraordinary expenses on bizarre decisions, including his insistence on shooting *The Room* in both 35mm and HD. The production dragged on for six months with significant turnover in cast and crew.

Lacking any professional guidance or oversight on his labors, Wiseau brought forth an incoherent screenplay that suggested he was afflicted with attention deficit disorder. Characters abruptly appear and disappear, bizarre pronouncements percolate without warning and are promptly ignored, and inane behavior (including a football game played in the street by the tuxedo-clad male leads) occurs without any explanation. The dialogue frequently degenerates into a skein of outlandish non sequiturs and after a while, it becomes difficult to imagine that the people sharing the scenes were actually having the same conversation.

Ah, but what is on-screen is utterly astonishing. Wiseau plays the San Francisco banker Johnny, although he looks and sounds like Dracula's grandfather, and Juliette Danielle is his unfaithful girlfriend, Lisa. Circling this couple are Claudette, Lisa's busybody mother—she casually announces that she has breast cancer in a single brief sentence and never raises the point again—and a somewhat odd young man named Denny, whom Johnny has supported financially. Denny might have developmental disabilities or he might be a drug addict—both hints are raised and neither is fully explored.

Lisa has become bored with Johnny, but Claudette urges her to stay in the relationship because of Johnny's wealth. Lisa starts hitting on Johnny's hunky best friend Mark and she then begins making false claims of abusive behavior by Johnny. Complicating matters are problems at Johnny's job. It all ends very badly, but then again, how could anyone spin a happy ending from this soap opera?

Fortunately for Wiseau, fate gave *The Room* a very happy ending. His 2003 Los Angeles release seemed destined to be a dismal failure despite an expensive marketing campaign that included an enigmatic billboard advertisement and promises of a modern-day Tennessee Williams-worthy story. As luck would have it, one of the very few people who saw *The Room* during its original run was screenwriter Michael Rousselet, who turned up at one screening to find he was the only person in the theater.

"It was like our own private *Mystery Science Theater*," he later recalled in an *Entertainment Weekly* interview. "I was calling friends during the end and saying, 'You *have* to come to this movie.' We saw it four times in three days, and on the last day I had over one hundred people there."

Wiseau would later grandly claim that his initial exhibition received enough positive feedback for him to arrange for monthly Los Angeles-based midnight movie screenings. Wiseau and several cast members would occasionally show up at these screenings, which began to take on

Rocky Horror Picture Show-style dimensions with audience members dressed like characters from the film and objects tossed at the screen. (In this case, spoons—Johnny's apartment had a spoon in a picture frame hanging on the wall; hence the cutlery obsession.)

Although Wiseau would self-release *The Room* on DVD in 2005, the production remained a midnight movie favorite in Los Angeles with high-profile fans including Paul Rudd, Jonah Hill, and Will Arnett. Over time, the film's popularity as a midnight movie anti-classic spread to other cities, then to other countries. Bobblehead figurines of the film's characters turned up in retail channels along with a video game. Many of the film's fans have lifted sections of the more ridiculous dialogue exchanges and grafted them onto unlikely videos, including clips from *Sesame Street* and a President Obama State of the Union address.

As for Wiseau, he observed the film's unlikely cult success in a characteristically opaque manner. "I don't ask you to like my movie, as long as you enjoyed yourself," he said. Really, who can argue with that?

Santa Claus
(1959, directed by René Cardona)

SANTA CLAUS IS A 1959 Mexican offering helmed by René Cardona, the filmmaker who gave us such epics as *Wrestling Women vs. the Aztec Mummy* and *Night of the Bloody Apes*. There are no wrestling women or bloody apes in *Santa Claus*, which is surprising considering what got into the film. This is the only Christmas movie I can recall featuring Satan, Merlin the Magician, black children dressed like cartoon cannibals, evil dolls in a musical dream sequence, and a computer with ruby-red lips.

Santa Claus eviscerates the traditions of Kris Kringle from its opening sequence. Rather than working from a North Pole factory, this Santa Claus lives in a ghastly arabesque castle on a cloud floating in outer space. And don't look for any elves here, either. This Santa clearly got inspired by Mexico's tradition of child labor abuses by rounding up a global collection of kiddies to make his toys. We know the kids come from different countries because everyone wears different national costumes and performs to what may be traditional folk music: American kids wear cowboy outfits and sing country tunes, Russian kids dress like Cossacks and perform a modified rendition of "Volga Boatmen," Japanese kids wear kimonos and sing what sounds like the theme to *Mothra*, and "African" kids wear leopard-skin loincloths and bones in their hair while jumping about to a bongo drum beat.

While everyone loves Santa (or so the narrator insists), there is at least one entity that despises the man in the red suit—another man in a red suit—Lucifer. Yes, down in hell there is tumult as Lucifer (presented as a disembodied voice booming over a torch) yells out his disgust at Santa Claus. Lucifer is so angry that he disrupts a hokey-pokey dance of demons. The demons are men in red jumpsuits with oversized horns and phony pointy ears hanging off their heads. If it sounds weird just reading about it, you can't imagine what it looks like on a screen!

Lucifer, determined to disrupt Santa's annual toy distribution shtick, calls for assistance from his chief demon, Pinch. Pinch agrees to go up to Earth to bring evil to the world's kiddies, thus upsetting Santa's Christmas Eve visit.

Strangely, Pinch's plotting of global juvenile delinquency is limited to a small section of Mexico City. He is successful in getting a trio of naughty boys to break windows and tell lies, but he has a bigger problem in getting a little girl named Lupita over to the dark side. Lupita's family is very poor and the poor kid doesn't even have a doll. Pinch tries to get Lupita to steal a doll and he even invades her sleep by choreographing a dream where a dozen human-sized dolls sing off-key and dance clumsily around Lupita and goad her to commit larceny.

But despite Pinch's pinching, Santa has secret weapons to ensure a successful Christmas delivery: a magic key that can open any door where Santa-ready chimneys do not exist and a flower that dispenses sleeping potion to hyperactive toddlers. Members of Santa's staff created these items: a shirtless blacksmith designed the key and Merlin the Magician grew the flower. Yes, Merlin! How he found his way from Camelot to Santa's workshop is never explained. And forget the eight tiny reindeer plus Rudolph. This Santa flies with four oversized mechanical reindeers that are wound up with a clockwork spring.

The kindest thing one can say about *Santa Claus* is that it is thoroughly idiotic and the insults not only go to the audience, but also to the title character. Santa himself is completely abused throughout the movie: he has a rock thrown at his head, he is knocked over by a flood of letters falling out of a mail chute, he gets chased up a tree by a dog, he gets his hand burned on a doorknob heated by Pinch, and is insulted when a child accidentally believes he and Satan are contemporaries. (Santa insists that Satan is "centuries older" than he is, but that his lack of physical youth is due to his "not feeling well lately.")

As Santa, José Elías Moreno is one of the least jolly St. Nicks in screen history. He goes through the film with wildly rolling eyes, flapping arms, and a jaw that constantly goes slack at the slightest indignation. It is difficult to determine whether the actor is having a cardiac arrest or is performing under the influence of a Dos Equis six-pack. You know something is very wrong when Pinch the demon is more cuddly and lovable than Santa Claus!

Santa Claus Conquers the Martians
(1964, directed by Nicholas Webster)

ONE DOESN'T NORMALLY associate Christmas with Martians. Of course, in a logical society, one wouldn't associate the birth of Jesus with talking snowmen and flying reindeer, but that's another issue, which this book is not concerned with.

And yet, Martians secured a place in the annual Christmas madness in 1964 when *Santa Claus Conquers the Martians* slid down the chimneys and into the projectors of theaters across America. Decades later, the film is still a source of wonder—basically, people are left wondering how such a crazy movie ever got made.

Santa Claus Conquers the Martians is a fairly simple tale. The kids on Mars are bored beyond belief and they spend too much time watching TV broadcasts from Earth. No, the local cable company isn't paying for the Earth shows—those darn Martians are stealing the programs! Anyway, the children of the Martian ruler Kimar begin shouting and crying that they want Santa Claus. The Martians fly to Earth, kidnap two children, and force them to guide the Martians to the North Pole. At Santa's HQ, the Martians and their cardboard robot spirit away Ol' Saint Nick while leaving Mrs. Claus and the elves stunned with a few ray gun blasts.

Santa and the Earth kids find themselves on Mars, where a new workshop is set up so Santa can make toys for the Martian kids. A bad Martian named Voldar tries repeatedly to eliminate Santa, but a good Martian named Dropo has a Santa fetish and saves the day. As a reward, Dropo gets to wear his own Santa costume. The Martian kids are too stupid to tell the difference between Dropo and Santa, so the Earth bunch are sent back home in time for Christmas while Dropo takes on a new role as the green Santa of Mars.

It is easy to knock this film, but in a way, it is not fair to criticize it too much. After all, the film was never meant for adults (although there is one adult joke when Santa identifies one of his reindeer as Nixon). *Santa Claus*

Conquers the Martians was originally designed for the kiddie matinee circuit. Way back in the days when neighborhoods actually had movie theaters, parents would deposit their children at the cinema on Saturday and Sunday afternoons while they did their shopping. These theaters would play films designed for the very young: cartoons, silly comedies, nature documentaries, and harmless action films.

Still, it is not hard to conceive that the kids of the mid-1960s were not going to question the notion of Martians being depicted by men in green greasepaint who wore capes, leotards, and helmets with antenna that looked like bent wire hangers. Or that these Martians flew around in paper plate spaceships and used robots that resembled cardboard boxes glued together and painted silver.

If the film sounds cheaply made, that's because it was. The film was shot in an abandoned airport hangar in Long Island, NY, for a mere $200,000. To save on their budget, the producers made liberal use of stock footage of U.S. Air Force jets as part of the sequence when the Earth attempted to fend off the Martian invasion. The same footage was actually used that year by Stanley Kubrick for the opening scenes of *Dr. Strangelove*, but it is uncertain whether Kubrick ever saw *Santa Claus Conquers the Martians*. (Though it would be fun to imagine that this outer space film inspired *2001: A Space Odyssey*.)

Santa Claus Conquers the Martians was picked up for release by Embassy Pictures and reportedly did wonderfully at the box office as an annual holiday release for the kiddie matinee crowd throughout the 1960s and into the 1970s. But after that juvenile circuit faded from social practice, the film vanished as well. It probably would've been completely forgotten had it not been for two unlikely events: the flick was cited in the bestselling 1978 book *The Fifty Worst Films of All Time* and it was cited again in 1981 when aggressive researchers discovered that Golden Globe Award-winning starlet Pia Zadora played one of the Martian children. Since then, the film became the darling of the lovers of so-bad-they're-good movies.

Another discovery helped bring the film to new audiences: there was no copyright registration on the title. Being in the public domain, *Santa Claus Conquers the Martians* was heavily bootlegged during the early days of the home video market. The bootlegging was frequently careless and some video copies were missing footage. The film gained yet another lease on life when the merry men of *Mystery Science Theater 3000* devoted a holiday episode to dissing Santa's trip to Mars.

Sextette
(1978, directed by Ken Hughes)

IN RECENT YEARS, societal attitudes toward aging have changed dramatically, due in large part to a shift in demographics that pushed the Baby Boomers into the realm of senior citizens. As a result, aging stars ranging from Clint Eastwood to Betty White are no longer viewed as candidates for the nursing home, but as vibrant and still very much young at heart.

However, attitudes toward the golden age crowd were somewhat different back in the late 1970s, which certainly explains the backlash over eighty-four-year-old Mae West vamping it up in her swan song flick, *Sextette*. Rather than viewing West as funny and foxy, most critics worked overtime to find ways of cruelly describing her advanced years.

Granted, *Sextette* is a bad film. But it is played with such ferocious tongue-in-cheek camp that its inanity has its own peculiar charm. And at the center of its commotion is the octogenarian West, still creating the naughty mayhem that made her a movie superstar back in the 1930s.

Sextette finds West playing Marlo Manners, the world's most glamorous and desired Hollywood star. This is perhaps the film's greatest joke and its greatest weakness. West, admittedly, was far removed from her *She Done Him Wrong* prime. As *Shock Cinema*'s Steve Puchalski harshly observed, "She's so heavily cosmetized that she looks like a Wax Museum reject; she sounds like someone Drano-ed her voice box; and she can barely move because her bones are so brittle."

In any event, West's character is on her honeymoon at a swanky hotel with her fifth husband, an English nobleman played by a pre-James Bond Timothy Dalton. His infatuation with her is so pronounced that they sing a duet of "Love Will Keep Us Together." However, their honeymoon is interrupted by a U.S. government agent (Dom DeLuise), who recruits Marlo to infiltrate an international peace conference going on at the hotel. If this isn't enough, Marlo is also distracted by the demands of her latest film—her hot-tempered director (Ringo Starr) and flamboyant costume designer (Keith Moon) invade her suite. And the men of the U.S. Olympic Team are also in the hotel's gym—a fact that Marlo exploits with an extended visit to admire the athletes' muscles.

To its credit, *Sextette* serves up a surplus of zany comedy. Starr and Moon go overboard in their respective roles and their overplaying is matched by Tony Curtis as a Soviet diplomat (complete with an absurd Moscow-on-the-Bronx-River accent) and George Hamilton as a Mafia gangster. The normally dapper Walter Pidgeon feigns vomiting as a peace negotiator who is served a lunch plate of monkey brains, while a somewhat baffled George Raft wanders about. Disco star Van McCoy and television talk show fixtures Rona Barrett and Regis Philbin also turn up, while Alice Cooper (as a bellboy) serenades West with a zippy tune. (Cooper originally composed a sad romantic ballad, but West rejected the song because she felt no one would believe she would rue the loss of a lover.) And for sheer weirdness, nothing truly prepares the viewer for watching DeLuise sing the Beatles' "Honey Pie" while tap-dancing on a piano.

While the all-star cast tries to steal the show, West commands attention—if only for her value as an elusive commodity (outside of a small role in the 1970 *Myra Breckinridge*, she had not been in a film since 1943) and for the unlikely spectacle of watching an eighty-four-year-old purr out sexual innuendos. When Dalton enters their honeymoon suite declaring, "I feel like the first man who landed on the moon," West wisecracks, "In a few minutes, you're gonna be the first man to land on Venus!" Later, West brags about her star power by announcing, "I'm a girl who works at Paramount all day and Fox at night!"

But there was a problem. Unlike her classic films, in which West seemed to be ad-libbing her bawdy wisecracks, many of her line readings in *Sextette* seemed wobbly and uncertain. Some of this could be attributed to age—her eyesight was weak and she was easily disoriented—but for the most part, West was forced to recite her lines raw with little or no rehearsal. *Sextette* was based on a 1961 play written by West, but director Hughes scrapped most of the dialogue and required a new script be written. But due to a rushed production, West was unable to learn the new script before shooting. As a result, she wore an earpiece (hidden in her blond wig) in which Hughes fed her the dialogue.

West's earpiece gave rise to a bizarre story from costar Tony Curtis that the actress once accidentally picked up a police radio frequency through the earpiece and began repeating the dispatcher's call while the camera rolled. However, Hughes vehemently denied that ever occurred.

The *Sextette* producers tried to gather support for their work through a series of publicized preview screenings in Los Angeles and San Francisco. West, who rarely made public appearances at this point in her life, gamely turned up and was ecstatic over the outpouring of love from devoted fans. Alas, it was not enough; no major distributor wanted the film and *Sextette* had a scant release from the tiny Crown International Pictures before disappearing from view. The $7 million production was considered a major flop, though West decided to pursue another film project with a big screen adaptation of her 1944 Broadway play *Catherine Was Great*. However, she passed away in 1980, leaving *Sextette* as her unlikely final bow.

Sh! The Octopus
(1937, directed by William C. McGann)

ONE OF THE WEIRDEST FILMS ever turned out by a major studio during the Golden Age of Hollywood was a fifty-two-minute 1937 B-movie comedy-mystery from Warner Bros. with the unlikely title *Sh! The Octopus*. And the title is actually the most normal thing about this utterly surreal offering.

Sh! The Octopus was based on a Broadway play that was staged in 1928. Why it took nine years for the play to reach the screen is not clear, nor is it certain why a full-length play was telescoped into a film running less than an hour. This severe editing, coupled with the inclusion of new slapstick sequences, created a work with a surplus of energy and a glaring deficit of coherence.

The film takes place in an abandoned lighthouse on a typically dark and stormy night. The lighthouse and the storm surrounding it constitute some pretty awful special effects: it clearly looks like a miniature structure positioned in a bathtub. The lighthouse itself has become the property of an artist, who is moved in by two demented old sailors: one named Captain Hook (complete with a metallic replacement for a lost hand) and one named Captain Cobb (who keeps babbling endlessly and is called "an old fool" by Captain Hook).

Meanwhile, in another part of town, dum-dum police detectives Kelly (baggy-eyed Hugh Herbert, who punctuates every other sentence with a high-pitched "Woo-Woo!") and Dempsey (Allen Jenkins with a severely dyspeptic frown) are driving through the rain when they encounter the lovely Vesta Vernoff, who is running for her life. Although it is raining with an intensity unseen since Noah's day, her hair and makeup are not the least bit dampened. Vesta fears that her stepfather, a brilliant scientist who invented a super-duper "radium ray," has either been kidnapped or killed by a crime boss called The Octopus. Vesta's stepdad lives and works in… you guessed it, the lighthouse.

The detectives and Vesta show up at the lighthouse and are soon joined by Vesta's elderly nanny, who answers to the name of Nanny. Why a grown woman needs a nanny is not apparent. There is also the arrival of Polly Crane, a wisecracking woman who claims to have been washed ashore from a boating accident, but she is also bone-dry despite the storm outside.

The lighthouse is a pretty strange joint. There is a body hanging from the tower that drips blood, but when it is cut down, it is discovered to be a straw dummy with a ketchup bottle in its pants. Lights go on and off, hidden doors open and lock, and every now and then, long octopus tentacles reach out from a dark doorway and grab someone. The octopus tentacles are operated by painfully visible strings and the actors work overtime to convince the audience that they are in a death grip. There is also a sea lion waddling about; the creature has no dialogue, which is a shame since he has the best screen presence.

All through the action, the two detectives carry on a running patter of bad puns, malapropisms, and some of the most thudding laugh lines ever shoved into a screenplay.

Dempsey shows off his brainpower by referring to a dead body as the "corpus delicious" and Kelly, when asked what he is doing in the lighthouse, responds: "Oh, a little lighthouse-keeping. Woo-Woo!" Those are the funniest lines!

Eventually, most of the people gathered reveal their true identities: the artist and the demented old salts are federal agents, the wisecracking boating accident victim is with a peace league trying to get the radium ray, and Nanny is really The Octopus… until the real octopus reaches its tentacles up from a cellar door and drags her to her doom. Just when it can't get any sillier, the film is revealed to be a dream that Kelly is having, who is in a hospital where his wife has given birth to twins. But why do the babies look just like his partner Dempsey? (Allen Jenkins plays the babies in a trick camera effect.)

Over the years, *Sh! The Octopus* has developed a very small but powerful loyal cult following based solely on the highly infrequent television broadcasts of the film. In one Internet forum, a seemingly endless number of discussions and punch lines have been laced around this weird little movie, making it something of a gold standard for cinematic lunacy.

Shanghai Surprise
(1986, directed by Jim Goddard)

WHEN REAL-LIFE COUPLES become reel-life couples, the results are often hit-and-miss. Humphrey Bogart and Lauren Bacall come to mind as the sexiest married couple in movies—even though they only starred together in four films (two made after their marriage). Richard Burton and Elizabeth Taylor saw their respective careers rise and fall in the 1960s and early 1970s as they pursued a series of joint vehicles. Other notable couples burn out before their collaborative work is presented: most notably, Orson Welles and Rita Hayworth saw their marriage fail before *The Lady from Shanghai* was released. Still other couples—most notably Paul Newman and Joanne Woodward, Hume Cronyn and Jessica Tandy, and Ossie Davis and Ruby Dee—enjoyed lengthy marriages and worked together on memorable productions.

Shanghai Surprise, the barely seen non-comedy and the sole creative collaboration from the ill-fated union of Sean Penn and Madonna, is set in 1938 China. Madonna, between playing variations of her music video persona in *Desperately Seeking Susan* and *Who's That Girl?*, took a huge leap of faith in playing against type as a chaste missionary nurse. The severity of this misguided endeavor was somewhat obscured by asking audiences to accept the rumpled Penn as a dashing, romantic, two-fisted adventurer.

The plot has something to do with Madonna's character trying to seek a shipment of opium—not for herself, but for medicinal usage at her hospital mission. Penn assists her in this zany quest, which has the inevitable tangle with Chinese gangsters who prefer to use the opium for less therapeutic purposes.

In the course of the film, the leads wind up in a surplus number of chases and fights, pausing only for wisecracking patter. The whole sorry story is wrapped with entirely predictable results.

Although the film offers handsome production design and a surprisingly strong music score co-written by executive producer George Harrison (who turns up in a surprise cameo as a nightclub singer), the effort is ultimately sunk by the painful miscasting of the charisma-challenged leads. *Fast Times at Ridgemont High* notwithstanding, Penn was never truly comfortable in comedy and he is visibly ill at ease in these surroundings.

As for Madonna, her incompetent performance in *Shanghai Surprise* secured her reputation as a no-talent actress and, to date, despite numerous efforts in a variety of vehicles, she still hasn't been able to shake that image. Fortunately, her music career never waned and her stardom remains as vibrant as ever. Penn, of course, went on to the proverbial bigger and better, snagging two Academy Awards in the course of his career.

Song of Norway
(1970, directed by Andrew L. Stone)

SONG OF NORWAY BEGAN as a 1944 stage show that was originally presented by the Los Angeles Civic Light Opera Association. Intended as a musical biography of Edvard Grieg, the production re-orchestrated the Norwegian composer's music with bizarre and clumsy new lyrics by Robert Wright and George Forrest; distinctively non-Scandinavian ballets by George Balanchine were also part of the show. Incredibly, this wound up on Broadway and later earned a trivia niche as the first American musical to open in London after World War II.

Song of Norway was quickly forgotten after its London run closed and it would probably have remained obscure had it not been dusted off amidst the 1960s rush to make movie musicals.

Norwegian actor Toralv Maurstad was recruited to play Grieg and although the forty-year-old actor was clearly too old to play the idealistic young composer, he nonetheless presented a fine singing voice and a decent screen presence. This was mirrored by an American singer, Frank Porretta, who offered a handsome face and fine voice while playing Grieg's artistic collaborator and best friend, Richard Nordraak.

Since neither actor had any box office cred, the film's producers tried to spice up the movie with recognizable stars. Robert Morley, Oscar Homolka, Welsh funnyman Harry Secombe, and (astonishingly) Edward G. Robinson were recruited for smaller guest roles. But the crowning coup was the film's leading lady: Florence Henderson. Newly minted as the star of TV's *The Brady Bunch*, Henderson found herself with the once-in-a-lifetime chance to outshine Julie Andrews in all the glory of Super Panavision 70mm and six-channel stereophonic sound.

So what went wrong? For starters, director Andrew L. Stone clearly tried to emulate Robert Wise's imaginative Austrian-based location shots in *The Sound of Music* by staging much of *Song of Norway* on location amidst the mountains, lakes, and villages of the Scandinavian kingdom. And, in fairness, the film offers stunningly beautiful travelogue-worthy cinematography that shows Norway at its finest.

However, *Song of Norway* was burdened with twenty-five songs and inevitably it becomes exhausting when people keep breaking into impassioned warbling and frenetic hoofing every few minutes. No location was safe from the songs: a hayride, a ferry ride, a snowball fight, and a chase down winding village streets inevitably turns into cause for belting out a tune or two. Norway was turned from a glorious land to an inane song-and-dance stage. And at one point, the film goes off into a fairy tale sequence featuring the cheapest animation imaginable—with Grieg's triumphant music used to prop up a bunch of cartoon trolls galumphing around a fjord.

Critics attacked *Song of Norway* when it was ready for exhibition. Pauline Kael was the most articulate in the critical denunciation: "The movie is of an unbelievable badness; it brings back clichés you didn't know you knew—they're practically from the unconscious of moviegoers."

Staircase
(1969, directed by Stanley Donen)

In 1969, 20th Century Fox presented *Staircase*, the first Hollywood release where the focus was on a gay couple's relationship. At a time when the depiction of homosexuals in the movies was limited to presenting gays as unstable and mentally ill deviants, *Staircase* was a giant step forward in concept—sadly, the film was a giant step backward for gay pride.

Staircase takes place in London's West End. Richard Burton and Rex Harrison play Harry and Charlie, a gay couple who've been together for three decades. The men run a barbershop (clearly playing on the stereotype of gays as hairdressers) and they live above their store. Harry's invalid mother, who is bedridden from arthritis, lives with them.

The duo did not grow old together gracefully. Harry suffered from an alopecia attack that resulted in the loss of his hair. To cover his baldness, he wears a turban made of bandages over his head. Charlie, the nastier of the duo, incessantly berates Harry for his appearance and masculinity—although a quick glimpse in the mirror should remind Charlie that he's no Steve Reeves.

Charlie's life is degenerating into something of a mess. He is facing a court appearance on the charge of performing a drag act in public, but he has no money to pay for legal representation. His daughter from his pre-homo existence is coming for an unexpected visit and he rudely asks Harry to leave their house and take his mother with him before his daughter arrives. Charlie's aging mother resides in a nursing home and she has never forgiven him for his relationship with Harry. When Charlie visits her to seek money for legal assistance, his mother brutally humiliates him.

Charlie further makes things worse at home by callously inviting a hunky young man home for a quick fling. Harry witnesses the arrival of the younger stud and locks himself in the bathroom, where he faints. Charlie manages to break down the door and revive Harry, worried that his longtime companion had a heart attack or a stroke. Alas, it was just a blip in Harry's blood pressure and he's soon right as rain.

Try to imagine every possible gay stereotype, multiply it by five, and you'll have some idea of what *Staircase* is like. The film is literally an endless skein of effeminate mannerisms, bitchy insults, immature and selfish behavior, and the chronic inability to offer a genuine romantic or affectionate emotion. At no time during the entire film do the male characters show any true signs of love for each other. There is a scene with the men in bed, but both are wearing loud pajamas and neither shows any signs of being capable of sexual arousal—the scene is clearly meant to ridicule the duo. It is hard to recall another film as epicene as this one.

Veteran director Stanley Donen helmed *Staircase*, but clearly had no control over his stars. Burton and Harrison ran amok on camera, hamming it up with atomic fury, and their off-screen lives further dictated the film's creation. Although *Staircase* took place in London, the production was based in Paris because Burton and Harrison wanted to circumvent the British tax laws regarding income earned outside of the U.K. Having to recreate the West End of London in a Parisian studio drove up the film's budget considerably.

A couple of unexpected artists were musically involved in *Staircase*: comic actor Dudley Moore wrote the film's score and Ray Charles performed the song "Life's Staircase." But even their tuneful contributions couldn't prevent the film from repeatedly hitting sour notes.

Starcrash
(1978, directed by Luigi Cozzi)

Long ago, in a low-rent Italian galaxy far, far away was the 1978 atrocity *Starcrash*. One can easily get a sense of déjà vu watching *Starcrash* because it slices and dices *Star Wars* with strange gender and species switching. This time around, Han Solo is a woman: Stella Star, the notorious intergalactic smuggler. While Stella may not possess Han's roguish charm or piloting skills (she gets arrested by outer space cops in the first fifteen minutes of the film), she has something Han didn't have: a killer body which looks smashing in a leather bikini and knee-high go-go boots. Caroline Munro, the B-movie goddess, plays Stella and the woman is simply a knockout—even Barney Frank would get an erection watching her.

This film's version of Chewbacca is not a Wookiee, but he is pretty wooly. The shaggy hair belongs to Marjoe Gortner, a one-time evangelist who became a sometime movie actor. Gortner was actually top-billed in *Starcrash*, although his role is actually a supporting part.

C-3PO is now Robot L of the Galactic Police. He is played by a man wearing a modified spittoon over his head and he is given a voice which sounds strangely like Yosemite Sam. There's no R2-D2, however, and no Luke Skywalker. But there is Princess Leia, who is now Prince Simon.

And while Carrie Fisher certainly knew how to lay on the camp in *Star Wars*, she was no match for the one-and-only camp regent David Hasselhoff as Prince Simon. Even in this early outing, Hasselhoff is a wonderfully ridiculous presence. He doesn't sing, nor does he go shirtless (that came later in his career), but he gets to flirt shamelessly with Stella Star in an overboard manner that is closer in spirit to Benny Hill than George Lucas.

In *Starcrash*, Stella and Akton are captured and sentenced to long prison spells for their various smuggling activities, but they get an unexpected reprieve thanks to the Emperor of the First Circle of the Universe, whose son, Prince Simon, has fallen into the clutches of Count Zarth Arn, who is trying to take over the universe. Get it, Zarth rhymes with Darth? Count Zarth looks more like Ming the Merciless from the *Flash Gordon* series, but never mind. The pair, along with Robot L and a bald, yellow-green man named Thor, zoom into hyperspace and wind up on several unlikely side trips, including a struggle with the Queen of the Amazon and her all-girl army and a bash with a brigade of hirsute cavemen. Don't ask how Amazons or cavemen got into outer space.

Besides ripping off *Star Wars*, the film also pays dubious homage to *Jason and the Argonauts* with a sequence involving a large statue chasing the itty-bitty humans (but this statue has pointy breasts) and there's also a riff on *Forbidden Planet* with mind-activated creatures similar to the 1956 classic's Monsters of the Id.

To its credit, *Starcrash* attempts to show some class with a couple of heavy-hitters. The Simon-less Emperor is none other than Christopher Plummer, who gives purple line readings to his anemic dialogue. Plummer seems to be in another movie with his impassioned and emotional acting. (The idea of Christopher Plummer fathering David Hasselhoff would make any geneticist apoplectic.)

Also slumming from the A-list was composer John Barry, who put this muck to music. Barry must have written the score while sitting on the toilet because it is the most constipated composition ever to grace a space adventure soundtrack.

Roger Corman picked up *Starcrash* for the U.S. market and sought to disguise its Italian roots by anglicizing the name of its director to Lewis Coates. The film was dropped in theaters like a cold meatball and Corman later tried to sneak it back in as *The Adventures of Stella Star*.

While Americans avoided the film, *Starcrash* did enough business overseas to warrant *Starcrash 2*, also known as *Escape from Galaxy 3*. That sequel never crossed the Atlantic.

A Streetcar Named Desire
(2005, no director credit)

WHILE IT MIGHT NOT SEEM fair to judge a high school student film opposite professional productions, an exception can be made for the wonderfully daffy (and totally unauthorized) version of Tennessee Williams' *A Streetcar Named Desire* which was created in 2005 by the students of Hickory High School in Hickory, North Carolina. Boiled down into a truncated half-hour edition, this film takes so many bold liberties with the source material that the Williams landmark is completely transformed from tragedy to comedy.

From the opening credit sequence, it becomes obvious that this is a *Streetcar* for the twenty-first century. Blanche DuBois is seen strutting down the streets of a business district, wearing a sharp white dress. She walks with an air of insouciance while the soundtrack fills the air with the old pop classic "The Girl from Ipanema." Meanwhile, Stanley Kowalski and his posse are seen strutting along a railroad track while "Bad to the Bone" blares on the soundtrack.

Blanche arrives at the home of her sister, Stella, and brother-in-law, Stanley. The Kowalskis live in a well-maintained condo development and their residence displays evidence of middle-class comfort (including a widescreen television and gym equipment in the living room). Stella arrives and she is wearing a polka dot dress and a wide-brimmed hat. The hat remains on her head for much of the film even though nearly all of the scenes take place indoors. Blanche spies a bottle of booze in the kitchen cupboard and the soundtrack inexplicably blares out "Pennsylvania Polka."

Stanley is not happy to have Blanche as a houseguest, or at least that's the impression he gives. It is somewhat hard to understand just what the teenage actor playing Stanley is actually saying—his garbled voice suggests that either he has a severe cold or is doing Buddy Hackett imitations.

Stanley hosts his pals for a poker game at his home. The all-teen cast is joined by a giggly preteen at the card table; the boys have problems avoiding eye contact with the camera and a few have problems keeping straight faces during this non-comic scene. Blanche meets Stanley's friend Mitch, who is played by a young man with a lean, athletic physique. Actually, the teen playing Mitch is physically right for the role of Stanley—the film's long-haired, muscle-free Stanley has a lithe physique that resembles David Cassidy in the early 1970s. This Mitch, however, is clearly aware of his appearance as the film offers a brief glimpse of the teen actor working out in the gym.

Of course, Stanley acts like a violent fool and pleads for mercy with an impassioned cry of "Hey, Stella!" If the Kowalskis are able to kiss and make up, Blanche is less lucky in love. Unlike the classic 1951 film version, this adaptation details Blanche's doomed marriage to a closeted homosexual. However, in this version, she discovers her husband's secret in a flashback sequence—as depicted here, she walks into a bedroom and discovers her mate standing five feet away from another man. The interloper looks at the camera, turns around, pulls down his pants, and shakes his bare backside at the viewer.

After that discovery is an extended dance sequence with several teens doing a wild two-step to "Pennsylvania Polka." The young actor playing Blanche's husband then abruptly runs off-screen, at which point gunshots are heard.

Of course, things get worse for Blanche, culminating in Stanley's sexual attack. This begins when Stanley slowly disrobes while "I'm Too Sexy" plays on the soundtrack. Mercifully, the grisly details of the rape are not presented: Stanley picks up Blanche, tosses her off-screen as if he was throwing a medicine ball, and then takes a Superman-worthy leap after her.

By the end of the film, Stanley's pals are back for another game of cards. Stanley sings "Coconut" while Blanche is chased around the condo by the people who are tasked to take her to a mental hospital. After Blanche surrenders herself to the kindness of these unlikely strangers, the film abandons the black-and-white format and switches to color for the last fifteen seconds of running time.

It is obvious that the film was made for a school audience: the brutality of the Williams text is erased by both the excessive editing to fit the shortened running time and by the polite nature of the acting. Indeed, the performances are so low-key that Blanche's cries of "Fire!" are delivered in the tone of voice that one associates with an elderly cat owner summoning her feline for dinner.

But this weird little effort, which emerged from obscurity thanks to a YouTube posting, makes such a zany mess of the Williams play that it impossible not to love its clueless and reckless style. Yes, the emotional devastation of the original play is steamrolled under a wild mix of inappropriate music and unintentional gaffes. But at least the young people behind this bizarre work deserve credit for taking the concept of creative license to inane new destinations.

Teenagers from Outer Space
(1959, directed by Tom Graeff)

TEENAGERS FROM OUTER SPACE OPENS with an alien spacecraft landing in a desert area of the American Southwest. A group of aliens who look like white men in bizarre jumpsuits exit their craft and begin measuring the atmosphere. But when a frisky dog comes by and barks at them, one of the aliens takes out a ray gun and disintegrates the pooch, leaving a canine skeleton. Another alien, a visibly young and strikingly handsome extraterrestrial named Derek (yes, Derek!), examines the doggie bones and discovers a dog tag. He quickly determines that the Earth is inhabited by intelligent life.

However, his colleagues aren't interested in that notion; they feel the Earth is a perfect place to breed gargons, a species that bears a striking resemblance to the lobster and which is the main source of nutrition for the men from outer space. The gargons supposedly grow to epic proportions, so the aliens decide to leave one chained up in a convenient cave to see if it will adapt to the Earth.

But Derek insists that bringing the gargons to the planet is wrong, so he attempts to start a mutiny. He is quickly overtaken and faces the prospect of a court martial. While the aliens are preparing to depart, Derek bolts and runs away. Another alien, a scowling thug named Thor, is given a ray gun and told to bring Derek back alive.

Derek uses the ID tag on the vaporized dog to find shelter at the address belonging to the dog's owners. Those happy folks are the beautiful Betty (Dawn Bender) and her tubby grandfather, who is known simply as Gramps. Although Derek shows up wearing a ludicrous jumpsuit and has no visible means of financial support, Betty and Gramps decide there's no problem in renting him a spare room that became vacant with the convenient college-bound departure of Betty's brother. As luck would have it, the clothing that Betty's brother left behind fits Derek perfectly.

The remainder of *Teenagers from Outer Space* is simply one extended chase with the ray gun-toting Thor hunting for Derek while Derek tries to stay one step ahead of his pursuer. Derek gets plenty of help from Betty, Gramps, an elderly doctor, a fat nurse, a none-too-bright reporter, and some of the stupidest police officers in movie history. There is also the matter regarding the gargon in the cave—it takes an unexpectedly strong liking to the Earth's atmosphere and grows to the size of an apartment building.

Much of the charm in *Teenagers from Outer Space* lies in the vim and vigor that reinforces its patent absurdity, particularly in the second half when the evil Thor spends too much time disintegrating everyone who comes into his path. British actor Bryan Grant sails into his role of the evil extraterrestrial with a scowling, visceral energy that one might associate with *Richard III* rather than no-budget sci-fi.

Director Tom Graeff previously created the 1955 feature film *The Noble Experiment* and raised fourteen thousand for this production. Money was so tight that a climactic alien invasion is never seen—the characters look up at the sky and talk about spaceships.

Incredibly, Warner Bros. picked up the rights to the movie, but the studio did not give the film a serious release. Instead, it was packaged with *Gigantis, the Fire Monster* (a sloppy U.S. dubbing of the Japanese *Godzilla Raids Again*) and dumped on the drive-in and grind house circuit before being sold to television. The film's odd title and its place in the genre of no-budget/high-imagination atomic age sci-fi ensured it would never be taken seriously.

At this point, Graeff's life took a very strange turn. He insisted that God spoke through him and he tried to have his name legally changed to Jesus Christ II. A series of arrests for disorderly conduct and an enforced hospitalization created embarrassment and Graeff was viewed as a pariah in the film world. Outside of an editing assignment on a 1965 cheapo sci-fi film called *The Wizard of Mars*, no one would hire Graeff.

In 1968, Graeff's attempts to advertise the availability of a new screenplay created problems when he made false claims that director Robert Wise and actor Carl Reiner were attached to the project. Graeff committed suicide in 1970.

The Terror
(1963, directed by Roger Corman)

***The Terror* was never supposed** to be made. Low-budget film wizard Roger Corman was actually in the midst of helming *The Raven* in 1962 at the cheapie American International Pictures studios when he realized that he was running ahead of his production schedule. Rather than waste the film's sets and stars, he contacted writer Leo V. Gordon about slapping together a script for a hitherto unscheduled film.

"I'll shoot on this set for two or three days," Corman reportedly told Gordon. "And that way, you'll only have to write the amount of script that we'll need for those two days. We'll stop the picture after three days and, at a later date, when we have a finished script, we'll film the rest."

Corman paid Gordon $1,600 to produce sixty pages of gothic horror material that could fit into sets for *The Raven*. The script was originally titled *The Lady of the Shadows* and Corman made a deal with Boris Karloff, one of the stars of *The Raven*, to serve as the new film's nominal star. Karloff received a small fee and the promise of a $15,000 deferred payment once the new production earned back $150,000.

Corman tapped another actor from the cast of *The Raven*, a young unknown named Jack Nicholson, to costar. Nicholson successfully requested that his then-bride, actress Sandra Knight, appear in the film as the ghostly presence that haunts Karloff's baron.

Unfortunately, Gordon's first swipe at a script was a bizarre hodgepodge involving a mad baron in the early nineteenth century (Karloff) who is living in an eerie castle. The ghost of his dead wife, whom he murdered upon discovering she was unfaithful, haunts him. A French soldier from the Napoleonic Wars who is separated from his troops (Nicholson, wearing Marlon Brando's costume from the 1954 epic *Desiree*) comes to the castle after seeing a young woman who may be the ghost of the baron's dead wife.

Since Corman only had Karloff for three days, he put the elderly actor through a rigorous series of multiple scenes. Karloff was shot walking down endless hallways and climbing staircases and he was submerged into a water tank for the climactic sequence that involved the flooding of the castle. Karloff was already in poor health when he began work on the production and was severely displeased at the direction he was receiving. However, Corman needed to get as much of Karloff as possible since the film began without a completed screenplay and it was unclear how Gordon's shaky foundation could hold up a solid horror film.

Once Karloff's brief period on the set was over, Corman found that his contractual obligations prevented him from devoting more time to the unfinished production. Disregarding Directors Guild policy, he turned over the direction to three young creative artists who were rising through the American International Pictures structure: Francis Ford Coppola, Monte Hellman, and Jack Hill (who also worked on the screenplay with Gordon). Even Nicholson was given an opportunity to direct several scenes. However, only Corman received on-screen directing credit.

Even if one was unaware of the backstory of *The Terror*, it is hard not to notice that the film is plagued with striking artistic inconsistencies. There are several scenes that are visually stunning—most notably an ethereal shot of the baron's alleged ghostly wife standing along a violent oceanfront and a jolting scene where a mysterious old woman hypnotizes the baron's wife with a multicolored magic lantern. But elsewhere, the film is full of cheapjack moments, particularly a cardboard graveyard that is home to a blatantly bogus crypt.

But much of the problem came in the form of Nicholson's blank performance and monotonous line readings. Filmmaker Peter Bogdanovich would later recall, "I remember thinking that Nicholson was a bad actor because of that movie."

Nicholson would later acknowledge that *The Terror* was a mess, claiming, "I believe the funniest hour that I have ever spent in a projection room was watching the dailies for *The Terror*."

Ultimately, Nicholson gave the best analysis of *The Terror* in a later-career interview: "It was incredibly bad."

The Terror of Tiny Town
(1938, directed by Sam Newfield)

SOME FILMS HAVE A VERY PECULIAR claim to immortality. In the case of this production, its legend is based on being Hollywood's first and (to date) only all-midget musical Western.

The plot of *The Terror of Tiny Town* is strictly by-the-numbers Western: a villain (played by Little Billy—and, yes, he is quite little) provokes a feud between two rancher families. While the clans are fighting each other, the villain plots to steal both of their properties. But a hero in a white hat (Billy Curtis) rides in on his Shetland pony to halt the feud, route the villain, and woo the prettiest gal in town.

Amidst the commotion are the usual suspects in these quickie oaters: a comic relief cook, a sultry saloon singer, a Stepin Fetchit-type black servant, and plenty of cowboys who don't seem to have any visible source of income, yet have plenty of funds to spend ordering beers at the local watering hole. There's also a penguin, for some reason.

There is also a brief appearance by a single full-sized person, an announcer who introduces the film and puts the cast in their diminutive perspective. But after the big guy leaves the screen, the film becomes a pint-sized alternative universe. (The cast averaged three feet eight inches in height.)

Of course, the lack of perspective dilutes the intended comic effect because everyone is around the same size. And while some sight gags are used to emphasize the cast's lack of height—the cowboys walk under the saloon doors rather than through them —the initial joke quickly evaporates.

Yet *The Terror of Tiny Town* is so patently weird and spirited that it actually becomes very funny (albeit in a perverse and politically incorrect way). The midget cast isn't especially talented and a lot of the dialogue reading comes across as hilariously stilted (the fight sequences are priceless in their clumsiness—obviously stunt doubles were out of the question here). And Nita Krebs as the Dietricheseque saloon singer is so wildly over-the-top (or under-the-top, in her case) that her musical siren call is priceless in its warped eroticism.

In case you are wondering why anyone would want to make this type of a film, the genesis of *The Terror of Tiny Town* was actually a casual joke. Producer Jed Buell overheard one of his employees bemoan the tight financial state of the film world by claiming, "If this economy doesn't turn around, we'll have to start making pictures with midgets."

Buell had hoped to create a series of all-midget films, but the meager box office return on this endeavor permanently derailed that notion.

Triple Trouble
(1918, directed by Leo White, with older footage by Charlie Chaplin)

UP UNTIL NOW, silent films have not been part of this book, mostly because the vast majority of bad silent films that have survived are just mediocre and not jaw-dropping awful. However, that's not to say that some astonishing atrocities weren't made before sound came to movies. This bizarre two-reeler is a mess on its own terms, but it has a truly fascinating history that makes its sheer awfulness all the more memorable.

From 1915 to 1916, Charlie Chaplin worked at the Essanay Film Manufacturing Company. During this period, his popularity expanded with unprecedented speed and he soon became one of the most famous people in the world. After creating fourteen films, Chaplin opted not to renew his contract with Essanay and, instead, signed a more lucrative deal with rival Mutual Film Corporation.

By 1918, Essanay's fortunes had diminished considerably. The cash-strapped Essanay could not possibly lure its one-time headliner back, so it opted to cobble together a Chaplin comedy from old footage and pretend it was a new production.

The Essanay staff found chunks of footage discarded from two of Chaplin's 1915 comedies, *Work* and *Police*. Also uncovered were scenes from *Life*, a feature-length comedy that Chaplin began but later aborted when Essanay complained about the production's length and budget.

Essanay entrusted one of its few remaining stars, actor-writer-director Leo White, to create a new scenario that would weave Chaplin's abandoned work into something resembling a coherent story called *Triple Trouble*.

Triple Trouble opens with outtakes from *Work*. The footage finds Chaplin as a janitor hired to work in a mansion. Edna Purviance is a maid who is charged with scrubbing the floors on her hands and knees, while Billy Armstrong (buried under oversized eyebrows and a beard) is the mean-spirited cook who has authority over the mansion's employees. In these scenes, Chaplin gets his hands all over the cook's food and manages to drop a can full of garbage on Edna's newly scrubbed floor. Chaplin picks up his mess, but Edna is upset and cries over her situation. Chaplin becomes tearful and wipes his eyes, forgetting that he is still holding garbage in his hands.

We then switch to new footage involving the mad inventor Col. A. Nutt, who has perfected a wireless explosive device. Diplomats from the nation of Pretzelstrasse want to obtain this device and the head of their consulate (Leo White) attempts to secure this explosive gadget. His dignity is punctured by having garbage dumped on him (supposedly by Chaplin's character) and then in the colonel's refusal to part with his invention.

The diplomat then encounters a thief on the street and they plot to rob the Nutt mansion for the invention. A quick-thinking cop overhears the plot and summons his comrades (who are shooting dice in a vacant lot) to take up guard in the Nutt home.

Chaplin turns up at a grimy flophouse for a night's rest. This footage was culled from both the unfinished *Life* and *Police* and it is easy to see why Chaplin jettisoned these shots: his vision of a grimy flophouse was too realistic in depicting the unsanitary deprivation of the flophouse denizens. Chaplin engages in bits of rudeness, including the placement of a burning match between a sleeping man's toes and the flicking of ashes into a drunk's mouth. There is an extended sequence with a thief (Billy Armstrong again) who helps himself to the drunk's hidden cash. Chaplin, afraid of being robbed, puts his money in his mouth and promptly swallows it. The scene ends up in a brawl that requires police intervention. Chaplin escapes by kicking a cop in the face.

On the run, Chaplin reunites with one of the flophouse denizens, who happens to be (surprise!) the thief engaged by the diplomat to rob the Nutt mansion. They abruptly return to the mansion, but the police get wise to the thief's presence. New footage is now inserted as a mad chase ensues with Colonel Nutt briefly being mistaken by the cops for the miscreant. The thief begins to fire his gun and accidentally sets off the wireless explosive. A massive explosion occurs, sending the cops into the air and propelling the thief across town and into the Pretzelstrasse consulate. Chaplin returns in the closing shot, peeking out of the rubble in an outtake from *Work*.

Triple Trouble never clicks because none of the Chaplin footage is even vaguely funny. Indeed, there was a very good reason why Chaplin never bothered to include the outtakes from *Work* and *Police* in those respective films: the situations were dull, the pacing was completely off, and Chaplin came across as lethargic and unengaged. Even worse, the new footage shot by White played like a third-rate Mack Sennett rip-off, complete with a lame imitation of the Keystone Kops running amok in the Nutt mansion.

When Essanay tried to dump *Triple Trouble* in theaters as a new Chaplin endeavor, the celebrated funnyman publicly denounced the film as a fraud. Bad reviews and even worse box office returns sank *Triple Trouble* and Essanay went out of business within two years.

However, Chaplin would belatedly forgive and forget Essanay by including *Triple Trouble* in the official filmography that appeared in his 1964 autobiography.

The Turkish Wizard of Oz
(1971, directed by Tunç Başaran)

For many years, the Turkish film industry was notorious for its habit of making unofficial remakes of Hollywood epics. These cheaply made films became masterpieces of campy, clueless inanity with rip-offs of *Star Wars*, *Star Trek*, *E.T.*, *The Exorcist*, and *Batman* as the most memorable efforts. But, hands down, the most remarkable creation of this wild genre is a film known to the English-speaking world as *The Turkish Wizard of Oz*.

The Turkish Wizard of Oz (also known as *Little Ayse and the Magic Dwarves*) blossoms into wholly unexpected and truly astonishing situations and sequences that recklessly shoves the L. Frank Baum source through the meat grinder. The film finds Dorothy, called Ayse here, as a happy farm girl with a cute dog who gets carried away in her house by a violent twister (depicted in excessively crude animation). The house lands on a witch wearing silver slippers (it would seem they don't wear ruby slippers in Turkey) which conveniently fit Dorothy's tootsies.

Whereas the Kansas Dorothy found herself in Munchkinland, the Turkish Dorothy finds herself in a wooded park where seven midgets dressed like toy soldiers sing and dance around her. The midgets have magical powers that allow them to disappear and reappear whenever the going gets sticky... and speaking of sticky, one of the midgets waves a phallic magic wand to conduct some heroic hocus-pocus.

Dorothy and Toto skip around a forest (no Yellow Brick Road here, just lots of nicely manicured lawns) and encounter the usual suspects, albeit with rather unusual changes in their personalities. The Scarecrow runs amok with a prissy personality that suggests the fussy old stereotype of a homosexual, although he is allowed an intensely brooding lament on his lack of brains with a soul-searching that recalls Marlon Brando's "I coulda been a contender" soliloquy from *On the Waterfront*. The Tin Man is found rusting and moaning in a strangely orgiastic manner and his humorless demeanor is worlds removed from Jack Haley's happy-go-lucky romantic. The Cowardly Lion has relatively little to do here but twitch his nose and the costume designer oddly covered his loins with an excess of fur that suggests the craven feline has a vagina.

In case you are wondering where the Wicked Witch is, she doesn't turn up until an hour into the film—she makes her presence known by blowing into a shofar. The Wizard himself, dressed like Merlin with a Gregg Allman hairstyle and shaggy mustache, also has the briefest of supporting performances and his balloon-ride departure from Oz is accompanied by a Dixieland jazz rendition of "A Hot Time in the Old Town (Tonight)."

Speaking of music, *The Turkish Wizard of Oz* abruptly breaks into clumsy song-and-dance numbers which are not helped by the obvious lack of singing and dancing talent among the cast; the score is somewhere between a Maurice Jarre knock-off and "Uska Dara." A village of overgrown dolls (played by children pretending to be robots) and a tribe of dancing cavemen (played by adults who should have known better) are also included in the mix.

The Turkish Wizard of Oz is so excessively strange and shoots off into the most unlikely tangents that the well-worn tale is given an eccentric second life. Sequences where the Scarecrow is disemboweled so Dorothy can hide from the witch in a pile of straw, or when the Tin Man is clubbed to near-death by soldiers swinging oversized boulders, or when the magic midgets fire a cannon at the dancing cavemen and spend five minutes laughing at their carnage brings a Tex Avery morphed into John Waters sense of nuttiness to the story which cannot be underappreciated.

Most amazing, though, is the leading lady. As Dorothy, Zeynep Degirmencioglu comes on-screen with supple breasts and painted eyebrows that suggest Turkish farm girls have far more glamour than their Kansas counterparts. Throughout the film, the magic midgets are constantly pinching and ogling her and even Toto gets into the act by jumping up under her dress. Dorothy also engages in some bottom-play with the Scarecrow, sewing up a hole in his rear end after he sits on a fire (but the silly Scarecrow only has eyes for the Tin Man with one of the most amazing flirtation scenes ever put on film!).

Forget Judy Garland… any guy who wants to have a hot time over the rainbow can hang out with the comely Miss Degirmenciouglu.

Valley of the Dolls
(1967, directed by Mark Robson)

NO ONE EXPECTED GREAT ART or emotional sensitivity from a big-screen adaptation of Jacqueline Susann's deliciously trashy bestselling novel about barbiturates-addicted actresses, but everyone was caught off guard by the garish awfulness of the much-ballyhooed 20th Century Fox film version. If anything, the movie did the impossible by making Susann's material seem stately in comparison.

The eponymous "dolls" do not refer to Barbie and Ken—they are 1960s slang for prescription drugs. And the valley where these dolls exist is the harsh world of show business. Falling into this glitzy trap is a would-be Broadway showstopper (Patty Duke); a blond looker who seeks a Broadway career, but winds up wearing next to nothing in "French art films" (Sharon Tate); and a New England cutie whose job as a theatrical agency secretary (Barbara Parkins) leads to a modeling career that attracts her to the entertainment world's sleaziest men.

While the film's over-the-top plot does not include having the proverbial kitchen sink thrown at these women, almost everything else gets tossed about: a spell in a sanitarium, an abortion, breast cancer, alcoholism, adultery, pornography, financial distress, and Susan Hayward screaming at the top of her lungs.

Valley of the Dolls was something of a cursed project from its beginnings. Despite grand pronouncements of major leading ladies in the lead roles—Lee Remick, Raquel Welch, and British singer Petula Clark were among the names cited—the casting was somewhat less than stellar. Patty Duke had cred as an Oscar-winning child actress for her performance as Helen Keller in *The Miracle Worker* and as a popular sitcom star, but this was her first adult role and it was uncertain whether she could make the transition to grown-up parts. Barbara Parkins also had TV stardom via

Peyton Place, but she was untested as a film star. And beautiful Sharon Tate was gaining attention in a series of small roles in films and television, but she was also something of an unknown quantity.

Perhaps to secure some degree of genuine star power, Judy Garland was recruited for the key role of the Broadway legend that feels threatened by Duke's plucky young character. Exactly what happened in preproduction is unclear; some sources blame Garland's emotional instability and penchant for self-destructiveness for short-circuiting her association with the film, while Duke claims that director Mark Robson intentionally kept Garland waiting endless hours in order to drive her to alcohol-fueled aggravation. In any event, Garland was canned (she would never receive another film offer before her 1969 death) and Susan Hayward came in as a replacement.

The tacky Susann book also defied easy translation to the screen. Distinguished novelist Harlan Ellison was among a trio of screenwriters hired to make sense of the script, but he was ultimately so embarrassed by the finished result that he successfully fought to have his name omitted from the credits. His collaborators, Helen Deutsch and Dorothy Kingsley, remained in the credits and absorbed much of the blame for the overheated dialogue and absurd plot twists.

Valley of the Dolls was first screened during a press junket held on a cruise line. Patty Duke would later recall the experience with horror. "When it was over, the cast was like rats on a sinking ship," she said. "Everybody went to their rooms, and many of us did not come out."

Rather than throw the film overboard, 20th Century Fox placed the film in a highly publicized release. The *New York Times*' Bosley Crowther summed up the critical reaction to the film: "It's an unbelievably hackneyed and mawkish mishmash of backstage plots and *Peyton Place* adumbrations… all a fairly respectful admirer of movies can do is laugh at it and turn away."

Despite the bad reviews, audiences came out in droves and made the film a major box office hit. But the commercial success of *Valley of the Dolls* did little to help Duke's and Parkins's careers and both women failed to find a niche in movies. Sharon Tate's career was not dented by the film's awfulness—her marriage to director Roman Polanski secured her A-list standing and her popularity was so strong that she received a Golden Globe nomination for *Valley of the Dolls*. Two years after the film's release, Tate was brutally murdered by Charles Manson's deranged followers; 20th Century Fox rereleased the film after her death and shouldered accusations of crassly cashing in on her tragic demise.

As for Susann, she went to court against the studio after it offered the 1970 comedy *Beyond the Valley of the Dolls* (co-written by Roger Ebert) production, which had nothing to do with her book. Susann died in 1974 and her estate posthumously won $2 million from the studio in a settlement.

Over the years, *Valley of the Dolls* found a cult audience that laughed itself silly over its strident soap opera machinations and badly dated view of the showbiz orbit. Not everyone found it funny, however, especially Duke, who felt her career was nearly derailed by the flick: "I always felt as if I was trying to redeem myself with each subsequent role," she said in an interview. "I don't know when the embarrassment from it stopped or waned, but it was probably not until the '80s. I think what happened is I finally wore myself out about it. You wake up one day and say, 'OK, I gotta find something else to worry about.'"

But Parkins would later join in the fun. During a guest appearance at a 1997 retrospective screening at San Francisco's Castro Theatre, she told a cheering audience: "I know why you like it. Because it's so bad!"

Visit to a Small Planet
(1960, directed by Norman Taurog)

ONE OF THE MOST INVENTIVE and wittiest plays ever produced on Broadway was the source material for one of the dreariest and least amusing comedy films ever produced in Hollywood. How did that happen? Well, funny you should ask…

The material in question is *Visit to a Small Planet*, written by Gore Vidal. The work originated as a one-shot production broadcast on the *Goodyear Television Playhouse* on May 8, 1955. However, reaction to the broadcast was so positive that Vidal expanded the work for the stage. The play opened on Broadway on February 7, 1957, and it proved to be a popular work with critics and audiences.

Vidal's work took advantage of the 1950s science fiction notion of alien invasions by offering an extraterrestrial intruder who uses wit rather than brute force to subjugate the planet. In this case, the urbane alien Kreton leaves his planet to become a spectator to the American Civil War. Alas, he is a century too late, but to his delight, Earth-bound warfare has progressed dramatically since the days of Lincoln.

Taking up residence with a typical American suburban family, Kreton decides to start a new global war strictly for his own amusement. "Isn't hydrogen fun?" he happily exclaims over the choice of bombs to employ. However, the Earthlings successfully appeal to his intellect and dissuade him from pursuing his plans.

Vidal's comedy offered a trenchant satire of Cold War politics and Eisenhower era social values. In both the television and Broadway productions, the droll British actor Cyril Ritchard embodied Kreton as an urbane, otherworldly presence. A highlight of the productions was Ritchard's telepathic communications with a Siamese cat—the actor brilliantly provided imaginative facial reactions to the feline's wordless repartee.

In 1959, film producer Hal Wallis purchased the screen rights to *Visit to a Small Planet*. However, Wallis would not consider Ritchard for the film version. Although Ritchard was well known to audiences from his TV performance as the zany Captain Hook opposite Mary Martin's Peter Pan, Wallis wanted a star that could bring in movie audiences. Instead, he cast Jerry Lewis, who was not exactly an urbane presence.

As a result, the film version of *Visit to a Small Planet* only possesses a shaky acquaintance with its source material. Screenwriters Edmund Beloin and Henry Garson removed the political aspects of the work, especially its acerbic view of the Pentagon's militarism, and changed Kreton from Vidal's sophisticated adult into Lewis's on-screen persona of a spastic, screechy man-child. In the film, Kreton is a student in a class on planet X-47. The student body consists of adult men who wear silvery pajama-type uniforms and Kreton is the class clown—he borrows a spaceship to go joyriding around the Earth. Although his teacher sentences him to write "I will not visit Earth" ten billion times, he sneaks off again in a spaceship and returns to Earth, landing in Richmond, Virginia. As luck would have it, he arrives at the home of a television broadcaster who is obsessed with proving that "flying saucers" do not exist.

The remainder of *Visit to a Small Planet* is mostly an extended fish-out-of-water comedy with the innocent Kreton trying to comprehend the Earth protocol. Since he comes from a planet where the inhabitants are not required to reproduce, watching how Earth couples engage in lovemaking fascinates him. He also tastes alcohol for the first time, resulting in his walking up the walls and across the ceiling. There is also an extended visit to a Beatnik club, where Kreton uses his telepathic powers to play the bongos in a drumming contest with Buddy Rich, which is then followed by a wild dance with a hot Beatnik chick.

In watching *Visit to a Small Planet*, it is impossible not to become depressed by the film's extraordinary waste of opportunities. The science-fiction premise is used to employ a number of special effects, but the gags are mostly silly (e.g. Kreton uses his powers to levitate traffic cops, Kreton hanging from a spaceship that blasts into the air). Even worse, Lewis surrounds himself with a number of genuinely talented actors (including Fred Clark, John Williams, Gale Gordon, Lee Patrick, Ellen Corby, and a young Earl Holliman), but insists that most of the funny business be centered on his character. As a result, he becomes the obnoxious life of a dismal party, especially in the grueling (and badly dated) Beatnik section of the film.

The critics, who were never kind to Lewis's work, were dismissive of *Visit to a Small Planet*—most notably, Howard Thompson of the *New York Times* dismissed it as "subtle as a meat cleaver." However, audiences in that distant era loved Lewis, the film continued his streak as a box office icon, and even the Academy Award voters got caught up in the action, offering the film an unlikely nomination for its less-than-spectacular art direction.

The Wild, Wild World of Jayne Mansfield
(1968, directed by Charles W. Broun, Jr. and Joel Holt)

AFTER JAYNE MANSFIELD'S DEATH in 1967, a group of exploitation filmmakers decided to cash in on Mansfield's death via thirty minutes of previously unseen footage of the star that was shot in Italy and France in 1964. Actress Carolyn De Fonseca was hired to narrate the movie in Mansfield's voice while weird new footage was added to create a *Mondo Cane*-style travelogue.

The Wild, Wild World of Jayne Mansfield opens in Rome with the star being chased by paparazzi as lusty Italian men pinch her ample backside. The pinched posterior is clearly the work of a body double—the real Jayne is shown in black-and-white footage while the close-ups of the rear end are shown in color!

Mansfield escapes this indignity to ogle the statues of muscular gladiators and then daydreams that one of the statues comes to life. And who should appear but beefy Mickey Hargitay, Mansfield's real-life hubby, in a clip from their 1960 stinker *The Loves of Hercules*. On the drive to the airport, she spots a line of prostitutes along the road who are welcoming their johns. The non-Mansfield narrator coos with a naughty, gossipy air about an Italian film star who supposedly began her career in this environment.

Mansfield then jets to the French Riviera, where she poses in the Marquis de Sade Fountain (the *what?*), dances the twist on a boardwalk while Rocky Roberts and the Airedales perform "The Bird is The Word," and sets off to a topless beach (she debates about shedding her bikini top, but opts to stay covered up).

The star then goes to Paris and all hell breaks loose. After getting a makeover at a salon (she keeps her heavy makeup on through the entire procedure), she hops on the back of a motorcycle belonging to a "Hell's

Angel from California" and winds up at the Eiffel Tower. From the structure's celebrated peak, the camera spies on a ribald Paris where everyone is having sex: a lumpy old man chases his lumpier wife around the deck of their houseboat, a dwarf and a midget visit a full-sized call girl at her apartment, and homosexual men cruise each other in broad daylight.

Mansfield then heads to the Parisian red light district (or at least the narration places her there, as the genuine star is absent from sight) and the film is then turned over to "Gloria," a British stripper who talks about the local adult entertainment scene. After a seemingly endless display of strippers plying their trade and a "Club Bust-Out" contest where women are judged on the best breast symmetry, the real Mansfield reappears for a lesson at Pierre's Striptease School. A clip of Mansfield stripping in the 1964 stinker *Primitive Love* turns up and proves she could unpeel her clothing like a professional stripper.

The film then heads back to America and Mansfield is supposedly the guest of honor at a "highly illegal" drag ball in New York. The film then swings to Hollywood and Mansfield discovers the town has changed: all of the women are topless. Yes, Hollywood is now home to topless women who work as ice cream vendors, auto mechanics, and shoe shiners. There is even a topless rock band called the Ladybirds.

Incredibly, the film follows up this surreal madness with grim reality: the news of Mansfield's death in the 1967 car crash. The fake Mansfield voice narrating the film gives way to a serious male voice intended to sound like a newsreader. The camera finds its way to Mansfield's Hollywood mansion, the fabled Pink Palace, where husband Mickey Hargitay silently and solemnly takes a tour of the now-empty house.

"A pair of shoes waits by the heart-shaped bed," intones the new male narrator. "Who will fill those shoes?"

Who would want to based on this mess of a movie?

The Wild World of Batwoman
(1966, directed by Jerry Warren)

WHO IS BATWOMAN? Her background is a mystery and the film offers no backstory. Her identity is a secret, too, and she is always seen wearing a large black mask. She is also seen wearing a strapless black leotard, stiletto heels, a fur piece on her right arm, a slinky cape, and a Patti LaBelle-worthy wig. Oh, she also has a bat tattoo on her cleavage. Needless to say, Batwoman stands out in a crowd.

Batwoman is based out of a ranch-style house in the Los Angeles suburbs. A small army of lovely young ladies, known as the Bat Girls, supports her. The Bat Girls don't have special uniforms—unless you consider bikinis and hot pants to be uniforms.

The Bat Girls offer their loyalty to their employer by reciting this mantra: "We the girls who are dedicated to Batwoman take our oath with all sincerity. We the girls who are dedicated to Batwoman take our pride with all sincerity. We the girls who are dedicated to Batwoman fight against evil with all sincerity."

The Bat Girls appear to have been hired for their dancing skills (which are considerable) rather than their crime-fighting skills (which, admittedly, require a bit more work to meet Gotham City requirements). This creates a problem when Rat Fink, supported by the German-accented Professor Neon, who is, in turn, supported by the dim thugs Tiger and Bruno and the moronic mute Heathcliff, try to steal an atomic hearing aid.

Yes, this is a real movie that was created by adults. And, not surprisingly, the "making of" story is just as bizarre as the film itself.

You might think *The Wild World of Batwoman* was the work of a raving lunatic, but it was actually conceived by Jerry Warren, an independent producer who specialized in importing cheaply made foreign horror films. On a few occasions, he directed his own productions and gave audiences *The Incredible Petrified World* (1957) and *Teenage Zombies* (1959).

Warren seized on the popularity of the TV version of *Batman* by creating this distaff riff. Katherine Victor, a B-movie actress who played Dr. Myra in *Teenage Zombies*, was recruited by Warren to star as Batwoman. She would later recall that Warren promised her an expensive action film shot in color. Instead, the film was a bare bones black-and-white affair with Victor creating her own costume. There was no money to create Professor Neon's monsters, so a few seconds of creepy creature footage from the 1956 sci-fi film *The Mole People* was inserted.

The film had to be retitled *She Was a Hippy Vampire* when D.C. Comics' legal team went batty over the film's title. (There was a Batwoman character in the original *Batman* comic book series.) But unlike the *Batman* franchise, Warren never created any sequels for Batwoman and her dancing Bat Girls.

Wizard of Oz
(1925, directed by Larry Semon)

DURING THE MID-1920S, comic actor Larry Semon wanted to keep up with his big-screen rivals by making the transition from shorts into features. Investing a considerable amount of his own money into the endeavor, Semon purchased the rights to *The Wizard of Oz* and set about casting his nineteen-year-old sweetie (and soon-to-be Mrs. Semon), Dorothy Dwan, as its star.

What happened next is one of the true mysteries of silent movies: rather than offer a straightforward adaptation of L. Frank Baum's book, Semon threw out nearly all of the story and created a production full of knockabout chases, pratfalls, a dungeon packed with pirates, spectacular aerial stunts, and heaping chunks of blatantly racist humor. For all intents and purposes, the film could have been called "The Wizard of Cresco, Iowa," since any resemblance between Semon's screenplay and the Baum classic was strictly accidental.

Wizard of Oz (it is also unclear why Semon jettisoned the article from the title) opens with the comic in old man makeup. He is a kindly toymaker who has created dolls to resemble the characters from the Baum book. His young granddaughter walks in and demands that the toymaker read her a story.

The old guy starts to read about intrigue in the Land of Oz, a strange place where the buildings have the onion-shaped dome architecture used on Moscow's St. Basil's Cathedral. It appears the rightful leader of Oz was a baby princess named Dorothea, who disappeared eighteen years earlier when she was an infant. In her place, Prime Minister Kruel reigns with an iron hand and the help of a dancing drag queen (really, don't ask after that aspect of the plot!). While Prince Kynd is leading popular opinion on bringing the long-lost Princess Dorothea to the throne, Prime Minister Kruel and his aide, Ambassador Wikked, decide to locate and eliminate their royal rival.

Meanwhile, in Kansas, lovely young Dorothy finds herself turning eighteen in a bizarre domestic situation. She lives on the farm with her saintly Aunt Em and her cantankerous, morbidly obese Uncle Henry. Courting Dorothy is a pair of silly farmhands—a small and stupid-looking bumbler (Larry Semon) and a pudgy, impatient beau (Oliver Hardy in his pre-Laurel days). There's also a black farmhand named Snowball who eats watermelon.

Unexpectedly, a biplane lands on the farm and five men wearing gaucho costumes emerge. It is unclear how they squeezed five men into a tiny biplane or why they are dressed like refugees from The Pampas. They demand a letter that Uncle Henry possesses, which is supposed to be delivered to Dorothy on her birthday. As luck would have it, Dorothy, Uncle Henry, the farmhands, and the men in gaucho costumes seek shelter in a farmhouse from an all-too-convenient twister, which blows them over a cliff (not over a rainbow, *natch*). Of course, they wind up in Oz.

The remainder of the film involves court intrigue as Dorothy and Prince Kynd manipulate around Prime Minister Kruel and his gang. The farmhands spend a lot of time in a dungeon full of pirates. There are several chases, including a daring aerial escape where Snowball flies back to Kansas with Semon hanging from the biplane by a ladder.

Oh, in case you are wondering about the Scarecrow, Tin Man, and Cowardly Lion, they are barely on-screen. The Wizard (who is depicted as a charlatan employed as Prime Minister Kruel's magician) disguises the farmhands in the costumes of the Baum characters for a few minutes so they can avoid capture. Yeah, that's it.

In lieu of Baum's timeless story, the bulk of the movie finds the star in anvil-subtle slapstick situations: getting stung in the rear by animated bees, being spit upon by a duck, falling down a hole, not realizing the phony Cowardly Lion was replaced in a cage by a real beast, etc. Semon mugs outlandishly at every indignity heaped upon him, which makes the gags even less amusing.

A lot of *Wizard of Oz* is difficult to watch because of the miserable racial humor directed at the Snowball character. He was played by Spencer Bell, who is burdened with the ignoble pseudonym G. Howe Black in the credits. While it was unusual for an African American to have a prominent part in a film of that era, the demeaning stereotyping (including a bizarre gag of having lightning bounce off Snowball's supposedly thick skull) speaks poorly of both Semon and the environment that encouraged such "humor."

After a successful New York premiere, the film's distributor, Chadwick Pictures, went bankrupt. Semon was unable to secure another distributor and theaters that booked the film were forced to cancel their engagements. The financial debacle ruined Semon's career and drove him into bankruptcy. As someone who was once considered to be on par with Chaplin, Semon found himself unemployable. Small roles in films and vaudeville engagements kept him active, but his health was wrecked. He reportedly had a nervous breakdown and was committed to a sanatorium, where he was diagnosed with pneumonia and tuberculosis. He died in 1928.

Zabriskie Point
(1970, directed by Michelangelo Antonioni)

DURING THE 1960S, Italian filmmaker Michelangelo Antonioni was the darling of the movie critics. His critically supported art house cred was so powerful that Metro-Goldwyn-Mayer signed him for a three-picture English-language movie deal. The first film of that agreement, *Blow-Up* (1966), was a major hit and earned Antonioni Academy Award nominations for his direction and screenplay.

However, his next studio project nearly resulted in the death of his career: the 1970 *Zabriskie Point.*

What went wrong? Well, *Zabriskie Point* is a hostile denunciation of a United States drowning in its own immaturity and cupidity. Nobody in the film comes across in a positive light: the college campus militants are pompous and vacuous, the police are brutal and stupid, the corporate suite is full of smug and self-possessed executives, and even little kids are presented as feral and ridiculous. The American landscape is even less appealing: polluted air, endless traffic, hideous skyscrapers, and tacky billboards covering every inch of free space.

Central to the film is the relationship between two lost young souls: Mark, a college dropout who steals an airplane after his shadowy involvement in a riot that left a police officer dead, and Daria, a young secretary motoring from Los Angeles to Phoenix on behalf of her employer, a real-estate executive trying to build luxury homes in the Arizona desert. As Daria drives down a desert highway, Mark flies over her in his stolen airplane. They eventually connect on an emotional and sexual level amid the dunes at Zabriskie Point in Death Valley National Park.

But in Antonioni's vision, the desert (a seemingly inhospitable location) is actually full of the mystery and vibrancy that has been squeezed out of American society. Alfio Contini's cinematography captures the strange beauty of Death Valley with stunning artistry: its sand dunes, rock formations, and cloudless skies seem more alive than downtown Los Angeles.

Death Valley is also the site of Antonioni's most astonishing experiment. As Mark and Daria make love in the dunes, the surrounding area suddenly becomes alive with other young people engaging in intercourse (they were played by the actors from Joe Chaikin's Open Theatre). Couples and threesomes roll and romp and grope with unbridled passion, as if they were spirits suddenly unleashed by the young lovers' emotions. It is a startling avant-garde moment that inspires awe through its sheer audacity.

Antonioni also dared to incorporate a harder-edged brand of rock music into the soundtrack. While the use of rock music in movies was hardly new, Antonioni specifically steered away from radio-friendly tunes in favor of a more challenging and disturbing sound. The director brought in music from Pink Floyd, the Grateful Dead, the Youngbloods, and Kaleidoscope; a tune from the Rolling Stones was also snagged. Oddly, Antonioni also became intrigued with the older pop standard "Tennessee Waltz" and went through an extensive (and expensive) effort to secure the Patti Page recording for a brief scene in a desert bar.

Sadly, *Zabriskie Point* is burdened by another Antonioni experiment that did not work: casting nonprofessionals Mark Frechette and Daria Halprin as the young leads. Frechette, a Peter Fonda look-alike, lacks the personality to fuel his role as a causeless rebel, while Halprin is so stiff that it seems like she is reciting her lines phonetically. The couple is great to look at when they are barely dressed and wordlessly making love, but once they are given dialogue, they are utterly lost. Ironically, a more capable leading man was on the set, but not recognized by Antonioni: a young Harrison Ford had an uncredited bit part as a student demonstrator.

Getting decent performances out of Frechette and Halprin was actually Antonioni's lowest concern. The production of *Zabriskie Point* was pockmarked with endless problems: the FBI reportedly spied on the entire production, citing Antonioni's politics as the reason for their surveillance; the U.S. Attorney's Office tried to halt production under the pretense that Antonioni violated the Mann Act in bringing the female performers to Death Valley for the desert love sequence; MGM cut out the closing shot of a skywriting airplane scribbling "Fuck You, America" in the air; and the studio added an inappropriate ballad by Roy Orbison at the end of the film because there were no MGM recording stars in the score (but no one bothered to give Orbison screen credit and his song was omitted from the MGM soundtrack album).

Zabriskie Point opened in February 1970 to hostile reviews. Roger Ebert sneered that Antonioni "tried to make a serious movie and hasn't even achieved a beach-party level of insight." Vincent Canby of the *New York Times* played the silly foreigner card by claiming the film "will remain a movie of stunning superficiality, another example of a noble artistic impulse short-circuited in a foreign land." And *The New Yorker*'s Pauline Kael sharpened her stridency by claiming the film "is a disaster, but, as one might guess, Antonioni does not make an ordinary sort of disaster. This is a huge, jerry-built, crumbling ruin of a movie."

The critics helped drive away audiences. With a budget of $7 million (a lot of money for 1970), *Zabriskie Point* grossed less than $900,000. The soundtrack album was also a major flop. Antonioni's reputation suffered badly as a result of the film's failure. Although he redeemed himself with the critics and audiences five years later with *The Passenger*, the final movie of his MGM contract, he never quite regained his earlier momentum, which was further halted by a stroke in 1985. By the time he was honored with a special Oscar in 1995, his reputation was solidified for his pre-*Zabriskie Point* output.

The fallout from the film also had strange effects on its nonprofessional stars. Halprin and Frechette briefly lived together in a Boston commune before splitting up. She married Dennis Hopper in 1972 (they divorced four years later) and she acted in one more film, *The Jerusalem File*, before pursuing a career as a psychologist and writer. Frechette left for Europe to act in two obscure films, then returned to Boston and was arrested in a 1973 bank robbery. He claimed his actions were in rooted in anger over the political corruption of the period. He died in prison in 1975 under mysterious circumstances (he was found with a 150-pound barbell across his neck—it was never determined whether his death was a homicide or an accident).

Over the years, some critics have tried to champion *Zabriskie Point*, but most reviewers still dismiss it as an aberration in Antonioni's otherwise sterling career.

If *Zabriskie Point* is a failure, then at least it is a striking and provocative failure that attempted to challenge audiences. And although Antonioni did not achieve what he intended, at least he made an imaginative effort to create a film that was different and daring—and, seriously, how many filmmakers can be credited for being bold enough to do something original?

About the Author

PHIL HALL is a contributing editor for *Film Threat* and the author of several books, including *Independent Film Distribution* (2006) and *The History of Independent Cinema* (2009). His film writing has been published in the *New York Times*, the New York *Daily News*, *Wired*, and *American Movie Classics Magazine*. He has also served on the Governing Committee of the Online Film Critics Society and is the programmer of the New England Underground Film Festival.

Phil Hall is also the publisher of Business-Superstar.com, an online resource for entrepreneurs. He has written on business-related issues for the *Hartford Courant*, *The Hill's Congress Blog* and *Progress in Lending*.

www.ingramcontent.com/pod-product-compliance
Lightning Source LLC
Chambersburg PA
CBHW062013220426
43662CB00010B/1311